PERSONALITY DEVELOPMENT for WORK

Allien R. Russon
Professor Emeritus of Management
College of Business
University of Utah

Harold R. Wallace
Professor of Vocational Education
Colorado State University

K42

Published by

SOUTH-WESTERN PUBLISHING CO.

CINCINNATI   WEST CHICAGO, ILL.   DALLAS   PELHAM MANOR, N.Y.   PALO ALTO, CALIF.

K42 Cover Illustration

The tree image is used because it represents graphically both change and stability. The tree itself—trunk and roots—is a symbol of strength; roots reach into the earth as we reach out to others for nourishment and support. But the outer leaf structure adapts to the seasons, as people adapt to, and are influenced by, their environment.

The color progression used in the tree's crown is based on the color wheel. Aside from being graphically pleasing, it might be said to show that quite different elements (or people, or aspects of personality) can readily merge into a satisfactory whole.

Library of Congress Catalog Card Number: 80–51989

ISBN: 0–538–11420–7

1 2 3 4 5 6 Ki 6 5 4 3 2 1

Printed in the United States of America

Table of Contents

iii

Introduction

Success in the world of work is based not only on your ability to perform, but also on your *personality*. In fact, in any situation requiring contact with other people—your family relationships, your personal and social activities, your employment—personality is an important key. To be successfully employed, you must develop your personality as well as your occupational skills. You must have the kind of personality that helps you make the adjustments necessary to fit in and become a member of a working team.

Two Dimensions of Success

There are two dimensions to be considered as you evaluate your success in the world of work. One is *efficiency*—getting the job done quickly without wasting precious time and materials—and getting it done right. The other dimension is your *personal satisfaction*. In addition to satisfying your employer, you must consider how well your employment provides for meeting your own personal needs.

Many psychologists have conducted research to determine the basic needs—needs we all have. One of the most prominent researchers, Abraham H. Maslow,[1] found that we all need to have shelter and food, to be safe and free from fear and danger, to be accepted as part of the group, to have a feeling of success and personal achievement, to feel that what we are doing is

[1] Abraham H. Maslow (ed.), *Motivation and Personality* (2nd ed.; New York: Harper & Row, 1970).

worthwhile, and to develop and use our natural talents.

You should be aware of the fact that both dimensions—job success and personal satisfaction—go hand in hand. It is rare, indeed, to find a person who is very successful and productive at work (especially over the span of a lifetime career) yet who is unhappy because basic psychological needs are not being met. Naturally, there will be times when you will find your work to be unpleasant. Even the most desirable jobs have some rough spots. And even the worst jobs may have some desirable features. But you should avoid the psychological stress—the misery—of enduring years of employment that do not help satisfy your basic psychological needs. Otherwise, your feelings of frustration and dissatisfaction will affect the quality of your work. Eventually, the backlash of your frustration at work will hurt your private life.

Personality and Job Success

Even though you may not be aware of it, you probably already understand how important a person's personality is in social situations. When you attend a public event or go backpacking in the wilderness, do you find yourself choosing your friends on the basis of personality? Of course you do. You choose your companions, at least partly, because you like their personalities. If personality is so important in the school lunchroom or on the tennis court, think how much more critical personality is as a success factor on the job!

One reason personality is so important on the job is that people do not have as much opportunity to choose their work companions. Another is that stress and pressure in the workplace can often cause conflict among co-workers as well as conflict between workers and their supervisors. Positive personality characteristics can help a worker to *adjust*—to get along and fit in. Negative personality traits can hamper or prevent that adjustment.

A person may be a "misfit" or a social outcast because of personality. When this happens the results can be very serious. The young, inexperienced person with little technical training will usually be fired or at least reprimanded. More highly skilled, experienced individuals may be transferred or given job assignments which remove them from the mainstream of personal contact. In other words, if an employer sees a worker as an important asset, a negative personality may be tolerated. But that worker will be socially isolated as much as possible, so that the others in the workplace will not be as affected by a negative personality.

Occasionally you may encounter an employer who will accept the challenge of trying to help an entry-level worker with personality problems. The help usually is in the form of a reprimand and a "second chance" to try to fit in. For those involved in cooperative education or work experience programs, the teacher-coordinator or training sponsor may try to counsel that person and provide constructive help with work adjustment—up to a point.

The Critical Personality Factors

When you realize how your personality contributes to your success as a worker, you will want to know what specific personality traits are most related to success. Also, you will want to assess your own personality to find out what you need to do to improve and prepare for successful employment.

Success-related personality factors can be identified because there has been so much research on the subject. The results of this research consistently point out several common personality factors as being important. A summary of the findings is presented in the following list of fifteen success-related personality factors. You should not think of these factors as single traits or characteristics. They are logically related "clusters" of personality traits. All of the most important traits logically fit into one of the fifteen categories. The major objective of this book is to help you understand and develop your personality in all fifteen areas.

The fifteen categories of greatest importance to success in employment are:

1. Ambition.
2. Cooperation and helpfulness.
3. Adaptability and resourcefulness.
4. Consideration and courtesy.
5. Independence, showing initiative.
6. Concern for quality of work, accuracy.
7. Carefulness, alertness, and perceptiveness.
8. Pleasantness, friendliness, and cheerfulness.

9. Responsiveness, ability and willingness to follow directions.
10. Perserverance, patience, and tolerance.
11. Emotional stability, poise, and ability to use good judgment.
12. Neatness and orderliness in appearance and manner.
13. Dependability, punctuality, responsibility, and reliability.
14. Efficiency, speediness, and productivity.
15. Dedication, loyalty, honesty, and conscientiousness.

As you study the list of desirable personality factors, do you see yourself being described? Possibly you are able to see some areas in which you are already prepared for successful employment. But you probably also see some clues about how you might need to improve your personality. This book can help you as you identify the critical personality factors which you need to develop. It can also help you highlight the strengths and weaknesses in your own personality.

Personality Development for Work is organized to concentrate in four areas. Area One provides specific suggestions for self-improvement in your *attitudes* and disposition. Area Two offers suggestions that will help you to evaluate and improve your *personal image* (how others see you). Area Three involves *communication*. In this area you will become acquainted with principles and techniques that can help you build social and interpersonal communication skills. Area Four offers constructive suggestions about how to increase your *productivity* through self-motivation, through better work habits, and through development of your analytical skills.

Allien R. Russon
Harold R. Wallace

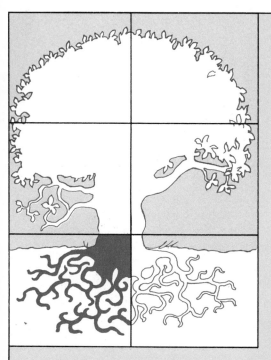

PART ONE

Inside yourself

Chapter 1
Understanding your inner self

Karen was assigned to help train a new employee, Greg, as they worked together behind the counter in a cafeteria. Karen took her responsibility seriously. She gave Greg detailed instructions on how to operate the cash register, how to cut and serve pie, how to arrange the vegetable and meat on a plate, and how to perform a dozen other simple tasks. Karen also watched over Greg, reminding him whenever he did anything wrong or when he chose to do something his own way. Can you see any possibility of trouble developing between Greg and Karen?

Is it important to understand your inner self? Yes, if you want to develop your personality and your chances for success in the business world—the world of work. To prepare you for your study of the following chapters which deal with developing your personality, it will be helpful to understand some basic principles. These principles are shown in a theory of personality which has been widely accepted. Possibly you will recognize it as the basis for something you have read in popular books or magazines articles. This theory, developed by Dr. Eric Berne,[1]

---

[1] Eric Berne, *Games People Play* (New York: Grove Press, 1964). See also Muriel James and Dorothy Jongeward, *Born to Win* (Reading, Massachusetts: Addison-Wesley Publishing Company, 1971).

3

Illus. 1–1.   Inside Yourself: Become Aware of Your Self-Image

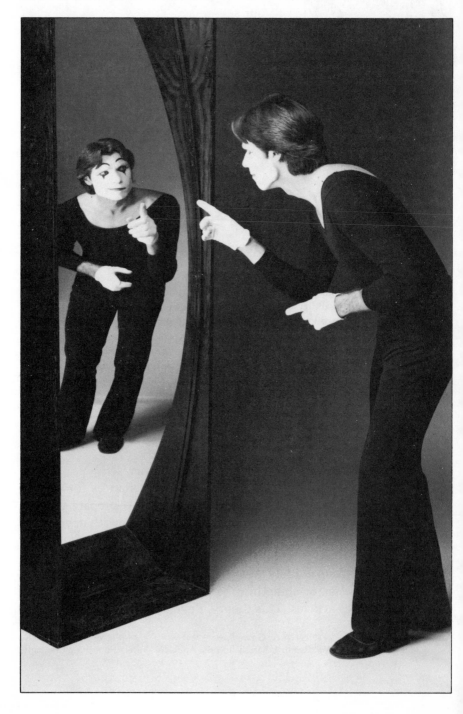

explains how your inner self—your "ego" influences your self-image. Being aware of your self-image—the way you feel about your appearance, your physical fitness, your talents, and all the things that make up your personality—is the first step in personality development.

A Theory of Personality

Your self-image is affected by three ego states, according to Dr. Berne. An ego state is the way you feel about something and the way that feeling causes you to behave. These three ego states are all present and operating in each of us. They are the Parent ego state, the Adult ego state, and the Child ego state.

When you act as your parents did, or as some other person who took the place of your parent, you are in your Parent ego state. Listen closely to what is going on in your head. Do you hear statements like these: "You look sloppy in that outfit," "You'll never learn to play the piano," "You are so stupid," "Don't drive so fast," or "This room is a mess"? If you do, your Parent self is operating. You are still saying to yourself the things your parents once said to you. In a sense, you have become your own parent. Unfortunately, most of these parental statements you are making to yourself (and to others) are critical.

On the other hand, your Parent self may want to take care of other people, give them advice, see that they do the right thing. Even though your intentions are good, the person you advise may resent it. The Parent in you may give others the impression that you are bossy, critical, or overbearing.

In the second ego state, you think for yourself. You can look at a situation, decide what the sensible alternative is, and act. When you behave in this fashion, you are being your Adult self; you are in your Adult ego state. The Adult ego state operates much as a computer does:

Computer	*Your Adult*
Data fed into the machine	You see, hear, and feel what is going on right now
Machine processes the data	You think the matter over
Answers come out of the machine	You act according to what you think is best

When you are behaving from your Adult self, you are able to deal objectively with facts, free from personal feelings and opinions. Your Adult self helps you to act from how you think, not from how you feel.

The third ego state, your Child self, is different for each one of you. The child you once were is still in you. When you are in your Child ego state, you behave in a childlike way. Some childlike behavior is undesirable after you have grown up, but some of it is good. The Child in you is the self that feels free, that likes to discover new things, that is able to be spontaneous. It is your Child self who can laugh and have fun. But just as no one likes a selfish, spoiled child, so no one likes you to whine or to sulk. Such childlike behavior *is* undesirable.

Figure 1–1. Your Three Selves

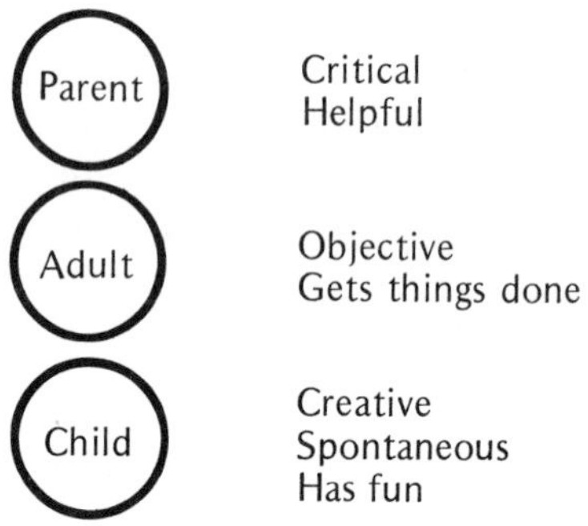

Parent — Critical / Helpful

Adult — Objective / Gets things done

Child — Creative / Spontaneous / Has fun

Your Transactions with Others

All three of your ego states must operate if you are to develop your personality, but your Adult self must be in charge. Your Adult self learns to listen to what goes on inside you. Your Adult self thinks things over and decides whether to use the behavior of the Parent or of the Child. The Adult asks, "Is this behavior appropriate right now?" The Adult self should drive the car, although the Child self and the Parent self are available when needed. If the Parent self or the Child self drives the car, there may be a smashup.

Much of the trouble we have in dealing with others comes from what Berne calls "crossed transactions." An example of a crossed transaction is the following: The sales manager asks, "Chris, when will you be done with the cost estimates on the

Billings contract?" This is intended as an Adult-to-Adult question. But Chris' Child self responds, "Why are you picking on me? I'll get to it after I type the invoices you needed in such a rush."

Figure 1–2. Adult-Child Crossed Transaction

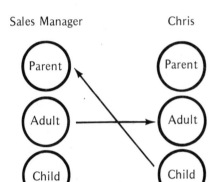

Let's look at another type of crossed transaction. The sales manager asks, "Chris, when will you be done with the cost estimates on the Billings contract?" Chris' Parent self answers: "You should know how much time it takes to do a job like this. Can't you see I'm busy typing these invoices?" Chris is letting the Parent self influence the transaction.

We've all been involved in crossed transactions, and we all know how uncomfortable they can be. When crossed transactions happen, we move away from the other person; good teamwork is impossible. When complementary transactions take place, however, the situation is pleasant. For instance, the sales manager says, "Chris, when will you be done with the cost estimates on the Billings contract?" Chris answers, "In about twenty minutes. I'm sorry about the delay, but I was interrupted by the rush job on these invoices." Chris' Adult self answered an Adult question. The Adult is in charge of Chris' personality. See if you can tell which of your ego states *is speaking* when you talk with someone. If you are careful to respond to the speaker from the same ego state as the stimulus statement or question, you can avoid getting into many crossed transactions

Figure 1–3. Adult-Parent Crossed Transaction

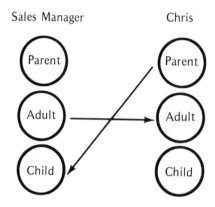

with the people around you. When someone speaks to you in a childlike way, answer in the same fashion. For example, a kidding statement is best answered with more kidding. If you take the kidding seriously, you are guilty of a crossed transaction. Also, if someone speaks seriously to you, you may offend that person if you answer with a "smart" remark. Just keep in mind *who* is speaking; learn to answer in a way that causes complementary and not crossed transactions.

Figure 1–4. Complementary Transaction

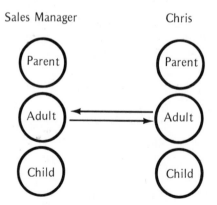

Illus. 1–2. Encourage complementary transactions.

Philadelphia Electric Company

Learn to Apply the Theory

What can you do if many of your transactions with others result in quarrels, hurt feelings, broken friendships? One important action you can take is to strengthen your Adult self. This involves three steps. First, you must understand yourself. This chapter is intended to help you with that important task. Then (as outlined in Chapter Two), you will need to develop your *self-esteem.* This means that your attitudes about yourself must be positive and constructive. Finally (in Chapter Five), you will concentrate on the personality characteristics that are important for success in the world of work. If you are successful in developing these characteristics, your Adult self will emerge as the most natural influence on your personality. Little by little you will find that you have built up a great deal of inner strength; small irritations won't bother you so much; you'll find it much easier to avoid crossed transactions.

Masks: On or Off

> Julie and Carol work side by side in the shipping and receiving department where mail is sorted and distributed. To Carol, Julie seems troubled. She does not seem to be paying attention to her work and occasionally she works very slowly. She often stands in front of a stack of mail while staring at the wall. But there are other times when Julie smiles and is pleasant. However, she never seems to sincerely share her real feelings with anyone. Carol tells you she would like to help Julie "come out of her shell and be a real person." What advice would you give Carol? What advice would you give Julie?

Do you wear a mask a good deal of the time? If you don't, you are most unusual. Nearly all of us hide behind a mask sometime. For example, we may dislike someone, yet we are exceptionally kind to that person to cover up the way we really feel. We may like another person more than we want to show; again, we hide behind a mask of indifference. Of course, if we did not mask our true feelings occasionally, the world would be less civilized. Politeness and manners are really masks in a way; they are necessary masks sometimes. If we always wear a mask, however, we are not likely to relax and feel good about ourselves.

You should have at least one person with whom you can take off your mask. You should have one person with whom you can be real—just plain you. That one person should be someone you trust and someone who trusts you. With that person you should be able to share anything: your fears, your hopes, your dreams—even your nightmares. With that person you should be able to be honest, completely honest both in answering questions and in volunteering information about yourself.

This friend with whom you can be yourself may be older or younger than you, the same sex or the opposite; it makes no difference. One psychiatrist has called this feeling of openness with another person "the transparent self." If you can be transparent with another person, there is an added dividend: *You* discover who you are. In fact, you do not really understand yourself until you have made some other person understand you. When you can talk freely and openly with another person, you will not feel so alone. You will have a friend with whom you can share the way you are, a friend who will accept you as you are. This kind of mutual trust and concern allows us to see ourselves and understand ourselves. An open and honest relationship will be better able to withstand the upsets that always come along.

Taking off your mask takes courage; it also takes practice. Start now. Find some friend with whom you can be your real self. Then you will gradually develop the strength to go without your mask more and more. A life free of self-defeating masks is a happier, more effective life. In addition, you will see and understand yourself as you really are. If you have an incorrect self-image because of masks you wear, you will find yourself working hard to live up to these false images and wasting much energy. Put that energy to work finding yourself. The "you" behind that mask is where you must start to build a success-oriented personality.

Illus. 1–3. Build a success-oriented personality.

American Family Mutual Insurance Co.

How Success is Achieved

If you are convinced that you should develop your personality, how do you go about it? If you should analyze the personal traits that make up a good personality, you might include a smile, a pleasant voice, a friendly attitude, the use of tact. These would certainly be some of the signs of a good personality, but what is underneath these surface signs? A personality can grow only when such growth is based on deeper personal qualities. For example, a genuine liking for people can have an impact on your success in personal relationships. If you like someone, you will want to put that person at ease. Doing this will make you forget your own ill-at-ease feelings.

Self-confidence—a feeling that you can do whatever you set your mind to—is another important personal trait. To develop self-confidence, you must do your best to excel. You will then have reason to be assured, to forget your inadequacies. Naturalness is still another good habit. To be natural you must avoid anxiety, for anxiety causes you to think too much about how you look, how you walk, how you talk. This makes you *self-conscious*—the very opposite of being natural—and reduces your self-confidence.

Building a success-oriented personality is not an easy matter, but it is a task that will bring great rewards. Personality is not achieved by picking up a few tricks. To build desired traits, you must *want* to improve; you must *believe* that you *can* improve. With knowledge and belief as the foundation, you can do the right things with a positive aliveness, and your personality will grow. The following steps will help you reach this goal:

1. Determine the type of personality you wish to possess and decide to develop within yourself those habits, attitudes, and traits that will best express that personality.
2. Keep in mind the image of the kind of person you wish to become. This mental picture must be so clear and so constantly present that your mental processes and your ways of conduct will bring satisfaction only if they stand approved by this mental personality.
3. Analyze yourself. Discover and admit to the weaknesses in your makeup. Face these facts squarely, then decide to remove the objectionable factors and substitute a new strength for any weakness that stands in the way of your reaching your objective.
4. Exercise the traits of the personality you wish to possess. Only by constant practice can you make these desirable traits a part of your ideal personality.

Questions and Projects

1. By what outward signs do you judge people when you first meet them?

2. The following test is designed to help you discover your own positive personality qualities. Answer each question by "Yes" or "No" on a separate sheet of paper.

1. If you make a promise, do you always keep it? (Yes   No)
2. If someone, a friend or a co-worker, or a member of your family, is in need of help, do you give that help cheerfully? (Yes   No)
3. Are you frequently witty in a sarcastic way? (Yes   No)
4. Do you have a tendency to gain attention by "topping" the remark made by the previous speaker in a conversation? (Yes   No)
5. Are you usually ill at ease with strangers? (Yes   No)
6. Are you critical of others when you feel they are at fault? (Yes   No)
7. Can you usually avoid being bossy? (Yes   No)
8. Are you able to avoid making fun of other people when they are not present? (Yes   No)
9. Do you frequently laugh at the mistakes of others? (Yes   No)
10. When others make mistakes (in grammar or in pronunciation, for example) do you correct them? (Yes   No)
11. Do you smile easily? (Yes   No)
12. Are you able to praise and compliment other people easily? (Yes   No)
13. Do you frequently try to reform other people? (Yes   No)
14. Are you able to keep your personal troubles to yourself? (Yes   No)
15. Are you suspicious of other people's motives? (Yes   No)
16. Do you frequently borrow the belongings of others? (Yes   No)
17. Do you enjoy gossip? (Yes   No)
18. Are you able to keep out of other people's business most of the time? (Yes   No)
19. Do you avoid talking about yourself and your successes most of the time? (Yes   No)
20. Do you ever use belittling words when referring to those who differ from you in religion, race, politics, or beliefs? (Yes   No)

If you are well-liked by most of your acquaintances, you will probably answer "Yes" to Questions 1, 2, 7, 8, 11, 12, 14, 18, and 19. Your "No" answers should be to Questions 3, 4, 5, 6, 9, 10, 13, 15, 16, 17, and 20. Give yourself five points for each answer you wrote that corresponds to the instructions given. If your total score is below 70, you need to work on more positive traits.

3. Keep a list of the times you avoid a defensive answer when you are criticized. See if you can strengthen your Adult self by agreeing with your critic. Evaluate the experience. Did you notice any helpful results?

4.   For one day, try to keep as many of your transactions with others on a complementary basis as you can. Try particularly to refrain from answering in a joking manner when someone says something seriously to you. For example, if you are paid a compliment, try to say something helpful to the other person. If someone says, "What good-looking slacks," don't say, "These old rags?," but answer more like this: "How nice of you to notice." Report on the results.

5.   How do you think an employer would estimate you on the following list of traits, and on what outward evidence would an employer base an opinion?

Are you	*or are you*
persistent	a quitter
sociable	unsociable
careful	careless
accurate	inaccurate
industrious	lazy
enthusiastic	indifferent
self-confident	self-conscious
ambitious	satisfied to "get by"
punctual	tardy
agreeable	disagreeable
optimistic	pessimistic
patient	impatient
thrifty	spendthrift
modest	vain

Case Problems

1.   Child, Adult, or Parent?

Bill Varner works in the business office of the firm of Strong Electronics. He has been working for four years, after graduating from the office administration program in an excellent community college. Bill's supervisor, Ms. Bartlett, was a kind, easy-going person and a comfortable working relationship developed between them. Two weeks ago, however, Ms. Bartlett was transferred to Baltimore and Bill was assigned to be supervised by her replacement, Mr. Kearny. Mr. Kearny is as brilliant and efficient as Ms. Bartlett, but he is somewhat short on patience. He speaks crisply and concisely to everyone. In Bill's anxiety to please, he finds himself making many errors. This fact in itself distresses Bill, but when Mr. Kearny criticizes his work rather sharply, Bill is deeply hurt and upset. He tries not to let it show, but this only makes things worse. Mr. Kearny interprets Bill's behavior as "immature." Finally, Mr. Kearny asks the personnel manager to transfer Bill to another office.

1. Put yourself in Bill's place. Is there anything you can do to eliminate this overly sensitive attitude?
2. What should a beginning worker's attitude be toward criticism? How about the experienced worker? Do you think being able to "take it" will increase or decrease further criticism?
3. If you were the personnel manager, would you tell Bill the reason for his transfer?
4. What suggestions, as personnel manager, could you give Bill to help him overcome his desire for perfection in everything?
5. Would you say that Bill is operating from his Adult ego state? Explain your answer.

2. Getting the Lowdown.

Joe Garcia has just started in his first job as a salesperson in the home furnishings section of a large department store. One of the older employees, Mr. Parker, asks Joe to lunch at the end of his first week in his new job. During lunch Mr. Parker talks freely and critically about the head of the department, the management policies of the store, and how hard it is to inject any new ideas. Joe agrees, adding that he has found it rather hard to work with Miss Green, the head of the department. "She seems to know all the answers," Joe says, "and doesn't respect the ideas of others. I guess she's afraid they might be better than her own."

The next day Joe is called to the general manager's office and berated for criticizing the department manager. Joe immediately realizes that his luncheon companion has reported Joe's comments. He is very angry and decides to be less friendly with the older employees in the future.

1. What do you think of Joe's solution to the problem? Can you suggest another solution that might be more effective?
2. What should a new employee's attitude be toward early friendship with other employees?
3. If you had been Joe, how would you have answered Mr. Parker when he criticized the policies and management of the store? Why?
4. Was Mr. Parker speaking from his Parent self, Adult self, or Child self? Explain.

3. Does Defensiveness Pay?

Sally Nelson has been very happy and successful as a junior accountant with Patterson and Lee, Tax Accountants. One afternoon in April, her supervisor, Mr. Mitchell, cannot find an important document connected with a case on which Sally has been working. He calls Sally to his office and accuses her of losing the document. Ordinarily a quiet man, Mr. Mitchell begins making accusations and threats against Sally. She tries to remain calm and continues to insist that the document was clipped with the others she had placed on Mr. Mitchell's desk that morning. In utter dejection, Sally returns to her office. Just before closing time, Mr. Mitchell comes into Sally's office and tells her that the document has been found. Apparently Mr. Mitchell had enclosed it with some other papers that he sent to another company. It had been discovered by one of the mailroom employees. Mr. Mitchell apologizes sheepishly and promises to avoid such a display in the future. Sally goes home and thinks the matter over. She has been unusually conscientious in her work, and her pride has been deeply hurt. Because of this incident, she decides to leave the firm and calls the senior partner, Ms. Patterson, the next morning to resign.

1. What do you think of Sally's actions? Discuss particularly (a) her calm when accused by Mr. Mitchell, (b) her decision to resign, and (c) her call to Ms. Patterson.
2. What was Sally's motivation for resigning from her position?
3. What other alternatives can you suggest in this case? Which of the alternatives, including Sally's decision, would you choose?

Chapter 2

Improving your self-esteem

"I'll never make it through this course!" These words, uttered in despair, greeted Carrie as she entered her dormitory room. Jill, Carrie's roommate, was enrolled at the community college in an accounting course. "I suppose it's because I'm such a bonehead in anything where math is involved." "You mean you think you will fail the course because you can't do the math?" Carrie asked. Jill hesitated. "I don't want to talk about it. I'll never be ready for the exam tomorrow, anyway. Let's go out and get a pizza."

It is not only important to understand yourself, as shown in Chapter One, but you must also feel good about yourself. Confidence and self-esteem can affect your success—or effect your failure. It seems almost inevitable that when you *expect* to fail, you *will*. But when you believe in yourself and expect to succeed, your likelihood of success is greatly improved. No one knows exactly why this happens. Possibly it is because your self-esteem influences your motivation. You simply try harder when you think of yourself as capable of success. On the other hand, when you fail, possibly it is because you betray yourself. You create the image of being a "loser" and this causes others to expect you to fail. Others may actually *encourage* you to fail without wanting or intending to—because you seem committed to failure.

Illus. 2–1.   Your Potential: Discover and Measure It

Whatever the reasons might be, a high level of self-esteem is almost certain to increase your chances for success in whatever you attempt. So, let us now consider some possible ways you might help yourself to build your self-esteem.

As you compare yourself with others whom you admire, you may decide that there is little you hold in common with such people. These people seemingly had special abilities that they developed. They made use, however, of what they had.

You, too, have individual talents. Discover them; employ them; develop them. What use are your own special gifts and talents if you ignore them? What use is a course of training if you do not employ the lessons it would teach? Do not blame fate if you do not make use of the powers and the abilities that have been given you.

Your mental attitude is of greater value than your mental capacity. Just at the time when you think you have exhausted all your resources, there comes a deciding moment demanding more of you than you think you possess. If you fail to meet the test, if you stop trying, you may lose the prize. A belief in yourself is essential to success; there must be such a sense of self-confidence and self-assurance that failure, no matter how often repeated, cannot get you down. The strength of will of the individual determined to succeed is an important factor in measuring success.

Do not expect that success will come quickly and easily; rather, be prepared to build it carefully and slowly. Profit by your unpleasant experiences, interpret them as opportunities for broadening your outlook, for displaying your own inner powers of resistance, and "keep on keeping on." Believe in yourself, in your ability, and expect success as the final outcome.

Discover Your Potential

It is as easy to find evidence of your potential for success as it is to find reasons to think you might fail. The key to success in life, and especially in employment, is to make the best possible use of the things you have going for you. For example, if you are tall, strong, and quick in your physical reactions, you might naturally choose to try out for the basketball team. For the person who might have other physical assets, other sports would be more sensible choices. When you consider the many possibilities—tennis, weight lifting, hockey, track, gymnastics, swimming—you can almost certainly find a sport that will allow you to use your special physical capabilities. However, if you are not at all interested in participating in sports, it would be a mistake for you to enter competition just because you might have the physical potential. Your interest keeps up your motivation. Your chances for success and personal satisfaction, therefore, are tied to your interest in doing something, just as they are tied to your physical capabilities.

If you are interested in music, creative writing, mathematics, dancing, auto mechanics, or gardening, the principle is the same. First, consider your interest and the motivations you feel from within. Then, take an inventory of your natural abilities and plan a course of action that will allow you to make the best use of those abilities.

Illus. 2–2. Discover your potential by listing and evaluating your talents and interests. Look for a career that allows you to use your abilities and that provides you with fulfillment.

If you are to be productive and happy in your work, you must first evaluate your interest and motivation as they relate to employment. Then, with an interesting and challenging occupation in view, you should take an inventory of your employment-related assets. Plan your career development so that you will be able to make the best use of your talents, physical abilities, social skills, and other personal characteristics.

Just as it is foolish to enter competition as a basketball player without considering your size, strength and coordination, it is also foolish to select a career without considering your potential for success in that field of employment. You should look at your potential in two ways. Ask yourself (1) *"Can* I succeed if I want to?"* and (2) "Do I *want* to?" In summary, your potential for success in an occupation relates not only to your natural abilities, but also to your interest. You might look at a career as having a potential for (1) allowing you to use your abilities, and (2) providing you with personal satisfaction and fulfillment.

When you discover your potential, you will certainly increase your self-esteem. As your self-esteem improves, your potential for success will be that much greater. Your enthusiasm, your positive outlook, your self-confidence, your motivation and general attitude, will be apparent to everyone. If you are a student, your fellow students and instructors will notice. There will be an effect on your grades. If you are employed or seeking employment, your co-workers and supervisors will notice. There will be a positive effect on their evaluations of your performance.

Measure Your Potential

In a consumer economics course, Howard found a unit on selecting and purchasing a home to be very interesting. As the class worked on a project in which appraisal, negotiating price, mortgage arrangements and financing were considered, he began to consider the field of real estate as a career. But he wondered, "Do I have what it takes to succeed in real estate sales? Are there strengths and weaknesses in my personality, my educational preparation, and my natural abilities that might help or hinder my success?" How might Howard proceed to evaluate his chances for success? How might he learn whether his first spark of interest in a real estate career is genuine and realistic?

Now that you are aware of how important it is for you to discover your potential for success in employment, you will want to know how to do it. There are several ways to approach this important task. You may choose to use any or all of the following:

Tests

Your school or college counseling office may provide testing services. Probably your community has an employment office which you may use. The names of these offices are different in various parts of the country. Some examples are *The Division of Employment and Training, The Human Resources Development Commission, The Employment Security Office,* and *The Job Service Center.* Most of these agencies participate in employment and testing programs under the supervision of the United States Employment Service.

Testing services can help you in your search for a job to fit your potential. Both seasoned workers and beginning students are assisted in finding the work they can do the best. Many of the tests measure characteristics that relate to the demands of various work situations. For instance, do you like detail? You may do well in clerical work. Are you a naturally orderly person? If you are, you have another clue that clerical work may fit your personality. Do you like to solve problems, work with mechanical things, work in encouraging relationships among people? Do you enjoy the challenge of variety and change in your work environment, or do you prefer to work with ideas? All these personal preferences can provide clues about the kinds of occupations in which you are likely to succeed.

In order to take advantage of testing services, you have several options. One of the best is your local U. S. Employment Security office. In addition to providing information about employment opportunities, this agency offers testing in the areas of aptitude, interest, temperament, and skills that are critical in matching people with occupations. Modern computer technology makes it possible to compare your individual profile of aptitudes, personality characteristics, and educational qualifications with similar profiles for hundreds of occupations.

Your high school or college job placement or counseling office may have similar testing services for you to use. Also, the information found on standardized scholastic aptitude tests used by most high schools can provide detailed information about occupational fields and levels of ability and aptitude in several areas. If you have the opportunity, you should discuss your aptitudes and interests with a school or employment counselor.

One of the tests that is most often used to evaluate a person's aptitude for various occupations is the General Aptitude Test Battery (GATB). There are no "right" answers for the GATB. You cannot fail this kind of test. Your highest aptitude scores indicate where your potential lies. Given a little help with the interpretation of your profile of aptitude scores, you will be able to visualize your potential clearly. This can provide solid evidence to help expand your self-awareness and confidence.

Many other tests, similar to the GATB, but focusing on a specific occupation, are also available. These Special Aptitude Test Batteries (in Electronics, Plumbing, Bookkeeping, Drafting, Auto Mechanics, Secretarial Work, etc.) can give you a more in-depth perspective of your potential for a specific career.

Counseling

Sometimes it helps just to talk to someone about yourself. A teacher, school counselor, employment counselor, relative or personal friend whom you feel comfortable talking with, can consult with you about your potential for success in employment. Often just the process of talking with someone can permit you to explore your feelings about yourself. This can help you appreciate the many positive aspects of your personality, your educational and experience qualifications, and your natural abilities. Usually, effective counseling takes more than just one casual conversation. Also, you may want to combine your counseling sessions with other self-exploration activities. All these activities should work together in a positive way to help you more fully appreciate what you have going for you. Most employment counselors will help you consider whether your interests and temperament qualify you for working mainly with people, with things, or with data. The process should help you appreciate your positive qualifications. For example, if test results indicate a strong interest in mechanics, you may say to yourself, "I feel good about myself because I know that I will do well in a job that allows me to work with mechanical equipment." At this time your self-image as a person who is talented in working with mechanical things is fresh and new. Next you will want to measure your potential with personal experience.

Try-out experiences

The best setting for measuring your potential and for expanding (or deflating) your self-esteem is in actual experience. For the athlete, the musician, the cook, the draftsperson, or the taxi driver, there are clear and obvious signs of success or failure. If you try your hand at mechanical work to test the validity of your new image of yourself as a person with mechanical ability, successful performance is bound to affect your self-esteem—to strengthen and reinforce it. The following example will illustrate this.

Irene was pleased, but a bit surprised, to discover that her mechanical aptitude score on the GATB test was well above her other aptitude scores. She had already made a tentative decision to "go into social work" as a career. To further test her mechanical aptitude (and interest) Irene spent three days in a career exploration experience, observing and assisting a plumber at work in a new housing development. She was fascinated to see how copper pipes were fitted together and sealed with solder. Irene was given the opportunity to "sweat a joint" herself. The plumber looked carefully for a flaw in the work, found none, and told her, "The inspector won't know the difference." Irene was delighted. Now she *knew* her mechanical ability was for real. She had discovered and measured her potential. Her self-esteem expanded. Her self-confidence helped her in an employment interview, and eventually she enrolled in a building construction management training program.

Another kind of try-out experience that can help you find and confirm your natural abilities and interests is to enroll in a course related to the field you want to explore. Some possibilities are adult education courses, community college or high school classes, apprentice training programs, and instruction sponsored by employers in business and industry. If you do not want to formally enroll in the class, you may talk to the instructor and students. You may be allowed to sit in on a few sessions and look at the course outline or text materials. However, you should be aware that what happens in a class may not actually represent what happens at work. This is especially true in classes that serve as preparation for advanced study. For example, a beginning accounting course may not reflect what it is really like to be an accountant. Also, there are many different kinds of jobs (requiring different aptitudes, temperament, etc.) for which accounting graduates may qualify.

Some other possibilities for testing your interest and ability and building your self-confidence before you fully commit yourself to a career are (1) career education programs, (2) involvement in vocational student organizations, (3) work experience programs (offered by education agencies or the Department of Labor), and (4) actual employment on your own. You may want to try your hand at a number of different kinds of work to see which you find to be most satisfying.

Your Improvement Campaign

Howard had made a decision. After reviewing the results of some aptitude and interest tests with his school counselor, he felt encouraged and more confident about his chances for success in a real estate career. When he visited with Mrs. Nelson, one of the top producing agents in the community, he learned two things. First, he *knew* he wanted to prepare for a career as a real estate appraiser and eventually as an agent. Second, he learned that he would need to improve himself. He was shy, somewhat afraid to be instantly friendly and outgoing, as Mrs. Nelson had been with total strangers. Also, he admired Mrs. Nelson's ability to present her ideas with logic and persuasiveness. Howard knew he needed to improve. What should he do now?

A desire for improvement is shown in your attitude toward your work. Motivated by this desire, you will welcome and encourage suggestions from your supervisors for doing your work more efficiently. You will be alert to suggestions for improving your work when they come from fellow employees. If someone tells you about an unconscious mannerism you have that is making you conspicuous, you will make a determined attempt to eliminate it.

No doubt you have seen the ads, "YOU, TOO, can play the piano, paint a landscape or write a novel." For your self-improvement campaign, let's borrow this phrase. *You, too,* can

Illus. 2–3. Improve your attitudes to attain your potential.

Pennsylvania Power & Light Co.

improve. It's guaranteed! What you must do first, though, is look at the current model very carefully. Imagine yourself as a product—the current model. Put yourself on the drawing board; analyze the product—you—in every detail. What are the good points? (Remember to always start with the positive.) List them. You will find that this activity will have a "snowball effect." As you write down one good point, it will remind you of another. After you have listed all your "plus" qualities, break them down into three or four categories. For example, you might group them according to physical appearance, mental abilities, and emotional qualities.

Now, take a look at the emotional category list, label it *Attitudes,* and check the traits that have room for improvement. It is best to start here because, believe it or not, you can talk about your emotional difficulties more objectively than you can about your looks or your brains. Somehow they seem more flexible, more capable of being changed. Because of this, you should feel less handicapped by emotional faults. For example, if you have a tendency to put off until tomorrow what should have been done today, you may tolerate this trait easily. It can be changed, however, if you *want* to change it. The fact that even though you are short, you want to be a basketball player may not be so easy to tolerate—and impossible to change.

These "born-with" traits, if you see them as undesirable, may cause a negative self-image which can be more difficult to handle than the trait itself. You must learn to adapt. You must learn to adjust. Sometimes you must learn to simply accept yourself as you are. The challenge is to be realistic. Recognize your traits, accept them if you cannot change them, and, as Chapter Five suggests, accent the positive traits.

From your *Attitude* list, select the trait that has the most references that are considered negative and is a trait which you feel can be changed. If you have listed procrastination, you may have also listed failing to take care of your clothes properly, forgetting to return library books, losing things, and so on. All of these faults might be lumped under the heading *Procrastination.* You put off giving attention to doing things as you should. This trait, then, would be the one with which you should begin your improvement campaign.

Take up another sheet of paper. There is a reason for this suggestion. We impress upon our minds the importance of an action or thought much more completely when we write it down than when we merely think about it. Thoughts are the most elusive phenomena we have. You may have a brilliant idea and think: "That's good. I must remember that." But what happens? You *don't* remember it! It fades away almost immediately unless it is captured on paper. In a similar way, writing down a list of things to be done is one step toward doing them.

On a piece of paper, then, write the title, "To Be Done Thursday," or whatever the next day happens to be. The best time to write this list is just before retiring. Below the title, list numbers 1 through 5. It is better to start with not more than five things to be done. Remember, we are encouraged by success, so make it easy for you to succeed the first time.

After you have written your column of numbers, write opposite No. 1 the most difficult, most disagreeable job you have to do tomorrow. Beneath that, write the next most important job, and so on down to number 5. Think hard about your list;

visualize yourself doing these things, perhaps in more than one way. Then place the list where you will be sure to see it the first thing the next morning. Taking this first step in conquering difficult tasks will help you build your self-esteem.

When you wake the next morning and are ready for the day, start on that first job. Do *not* do all of the short, easy jobs first. You may think that you will finish the easy jobs first so that you will have nothing else on your mind and can concentrate on the big job. This is a fallacy. When you finish the short, easy jobs, you will have *nothing* on your mind. You will be tired and will probably decide to wait until tomorrow to get at that hard job.

After item No. 1 is finished, begin No. 2, and upon completion of the task, begin the next one. You may not finish all the items on the list, but that is all right. The most difficult job has been finished, and you should give yourself the heartiest of congratulations. Forget the items at the bottom of the list that you did not reach, and just add them to the next day's list. Concentrate on what you *did* do, not what you *did not* do.

One specific approach to self-improvement that has been successful for many people is to use *behavior modification*. Behavior modification is a procedure for causing behavior change through application of well-known principles of psychology. These principles involve the use of reward and punishment. If you are going to use behavior modification to change yourself, you will first need to have your own system of rewards. You may like to take your car apart and put it back together again; or you may prefer to listen to music or sit in a quiet corner and read a favorite book. The thing to do is to think about *you*. What do you like to do best? Take a piece of paper and write down 10 to 20 activities that you enjoy. Of course, these activities must be possible in your present circumstances. You can't say you would like to spend a million dollars because you don't have a million dollars. Just write down the activities you enjoy most, the ones that are possible right now.

When you have your list of rewards drawn up, draw up a contract. You promise yourself that you are going to change in some way. You may decide to study more effectively. You may decide to control your bad temper. Whatever your behavior change is going to be, write it down. Then set up a system of rewards. If you follow your program of change for one hour, you get a certain reward. If you continue for an entire day, you get a better reward, and so on. But remember: the reward is important—just as important as the change in your behavior. If you fail to give yourself the reward, you will stop trying to improve.

Of all the many factors that influence a person's success, probably the most important is self-esteem. You can improve your self-esteem by following the suggestions outlined in this chapter—discovering your potential, measuring it, and working to improve it. Your improvement campaign will pay off in greater motivation and greater personal satisfaction. As you see what you are able to accomplish, your self-esteem will increase even more. So, if you work at it, each new cycle of self-improvement will propel you to higher levels of self-esteem, motivation, and satisfaction.

Questions and Projects

1. Interview an experienced worker in a job that you would like to have. Ask this worker to tell you something about the qualities needed for the job, the personality traits that are aids to success, and something about the standards of work.

2. Interview a business executive. Take notes on all that is told you. Ask questions to determine the type of employee wanted by the business.

3. Office work is competitive. How will you compare with other applicants for the job you want? On a separate sheet of paper, rate yourself on the following qualities using these numbers: 3—very good; 2—average; and 1—poor.

Reliability	Manners	Leadership
Good nature	Poise	Intelligence
Honesty	Concentration	Accuracy

Now rate three of your friends who are also ready to look for their first jobs. Be honest—and do not refer to your own scores, then compare yourself with your friends. If you score higher, you are probably ready for employment. If you score lower, you have more work to do.

4. On a form like that below, keep an up-to-date list of suggestions you encounter in your work and in your reading that you think might help you to grow. Place a check (√) beside each suggestion that you try out. If you find the suggestion helpful, put a second check mark beside the first one.

Suggestion	√	√

5. We all have mental pictures of ourselves. Sometimes they are good likenesses and sometimes they are not. On a grid like the one shown below, place a check in Column 1 next to the statements that correspond to what you think you are like. In Column 2, on your grid, check the statements you believe other people think you are like. In Column 3, check the statement you would most like to be someday.

a. *How I Feel About Myself*

	1	2	3
Inferior to most of my associates			
Superior to most of my associates			
Self-confident			
Lacking self-confidence			
Proud of my achievements			
Modest about my achievements			
Conceited about my appearance			
Ashamed of my appearance			

b. *How I Feel Toward Others*

	1	2	3
Tolerant			
Intolerant			
Friendly			
Unfriendly			
Like to be with others			
Dislike to be with others			
Like most people			
Dislike most people			

6. Psychologists say that we become what we think. As part of your improvement campaign, try keeping an improved mental picture of yourself in mind. Write down the statements from Column No. 3 (in No. 5) that indicate what you would like to be someday. Visualize yourself as being this way for the next three months. At the end of that time, try this rating again. The results may be a pleasant surprise to you.

Case Problems

1. Dead End?

Dick Ellsworth majored in secretarial science at a two-year business college. After he graduated, he tried for several weeks to find a job as a private secretary, but with no success. Finally, he found a job as a clerk-typist in a large life insurance company. He has been working now for nearly a year. His supervisor is pleased with his work. While Dick's salary is not large, he has had two raises in the last six months. The physical benefits in the office are extremely good; there are also many fringe benefits that are attractive. The routine work he is doing, however, is below his abilities. While attending school, Dick did extremely well in shorthand and simulated office procedures. Now, he fears he will lose his shorthand speed because of lack of practice.

1. Put yourself in Dick's place. What are some of the possible solutions to the problem?
2. After evaluating the possible solutions, which ones would you choose?

2. Short- or Long-Term Goals?

Patrick had always wanted to be a lawyer. Both his mother and grandfather had been attorneys, and Patrick had always been certain of his career. After three years of college, however, he was told that his grades were not high enough for him to be accepted by law school. Patrick's schoolwork slipped badly after this news, and his counselor, Miss Cannon, called him in for an interview. During the interview, Patrick told Miss Cannon that he had no other interests. He added, "If I can't be a lawyer, I won't be anything." At this point, Miss Cannon asked about the other courses Patrick had taken in high school and college.

Among other things, Patrick mentioned that he had taken typing and shorthand in high school and had reached a high level of skill in both subjects. Miss Cannon then suggested that Patrick find a part-time job as a secretary in a law office while taking a reduced load in college.

1. What advantages to Patrick do you see in this suggestion?
2. Will firsthand knowledge of legal work give Patrick a more realistic idea of his goal?
3. What effect do you think working part-time will have on Patrick's grades in college? Why?
4. Do you think working as a legal secretary may help if he is later accepted in a school of law?

3. Start at the Top?

Mr. Harwood, the vocational counselor at Lincoln High School, asked Lynn to apply for a job as general clerk with the A-One Trucking Company. Lynn had just graduated and she was well qualified for the work. She got the job. The salary was good and the supervisor was fair, but after a month Lynn quit her job. She told Mr. Harwood that she could have stayed on the job forever and never would have had a chance to do anything but what she had done every day for a month—routing, checking, and keeping routine records.

Mr. Harwood called to check with Mr. Wellington, the owner of the A-One Trucking Company, to see what was wrong. Mr. Wellington said, "Too anxious to be vice-president. Lynn told me she didn't see how she could get anywhere in this business. She wanted to get ahead too fast. She couldn't see the chance was right here waiting for her."

1. Do you agree with Lynn's attitude about getting ahead? Why or why not?
2. How long should it take in a new position before an employee is worth the salary?
3. Do you think any vocation or profession is free from drudgery?
4. If you were a beginning worker, what would be your attitude toward routine work?

4. It Works Both Ways.

Joan is desperate to find a job to support her family. She hears of a job in a box factory and applies at once. She is interviewed by one of the company officers and is given a series of tests. The following day, Mrs. Daynes, the person who interviewed Joan, calls her and says she has not been given the job because her test scores were too high. Joan insists that she would be happy to take the job, no matter what the test scores say. Mrs. Daynes insists, however, that it is company policy to give routine, repetitive jobs only to applicants of average ability. Joan feels that she has been treated unfairly.

1. Why should such a policy be made? What is its purpose?
2. Do you agree that Joan might not enjoy working at repetitive, monotonous work?
3. What should Joan do now? Is there any place she can go for further advice?
4. What other policies can you suggest for dealing with this problem of repetition?

5. Are You a Team Worker?

Maxine has been a brilliant student in high school and college, but has never shown an interest in school activities. There are two jobs open in the Peerless Bonding Company. One requires that the individual be able to work with others and prefer this type of work to that done alone. The other job is an actuarial job which allows the individual to work alone. When the head of the firm, Mr. Kenny, interviews Maxine, he suggests that the actuarial job, requiring no group work, might be the better choice for Maxine. This suggestion is agreeable to Maxine, but she wonders how Mr. Kenny was aware of her preference.

1. Do you agree with Mr. Kenny that participation in school activities indicates a liking for people?
2. What jobs can you list that require team effort?
3. Which ones can you list that need no ability to work with others?
4. Which of your lists is the longer? What does this fact indicate?

6. Room at the Top?

Tad has obtained a subordinate position in an advertising firm. In high school Tad capably handled all the advertising copy for the various school publications. He feels, therefore, that his experience fits him for doing creative work, and he is not interested in the tasks assigned to him. He considers them to be dull, routine duties. The manager knows that because Tad cannot do the type of work he wants to do, he often neglects to do well the work he has to do. Tad's negligence also causes more work for others in the office. They, in turn, complain to the manager. When Tad is called to the manager for questioning, he explains that he does not like his present tasks and tells of his ambition. She does not seem to be impressed with his reasoning.

1. What is your opinion of Tad's attitude toward his work?
2. If you were the manager, what would you say to Tad?
3. Why did Tad's ambition fail to impress the manager?
4. Have you observed this attitude toward starting at the bottom in other lines of work? Explain.
5. Why was Tad's attitude not fair to the other employees?

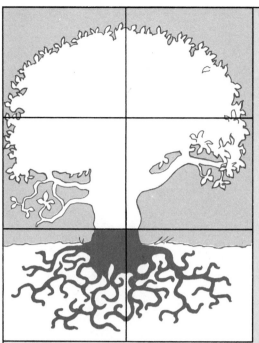

PART TWO
Outside yourself

Chapter 3
Personal appearance and health

The first two chapters of this book have been concerned with your inner self. We have discussed your self-understanding and self-esteem, how to develop positive attitudes, and the effects of your own standards of conduct on your success in the world of work. All these personality characteristics are very important. Now we will begin to look at the more obvious, more visible aspects of your personality. Personality is not only the inner (invisible) characteristics described earlier. It is also what people see—your personal appearance. It is also how you feel physically. In this chapter we will discuss the personality that people see: your health, your dress and grooming.

Your Health Is Showing

> Joe often comes to work looking as though he only had a couple of hours of sleep the night before. His clothes are wrinkled and frequently are stained. He usually grabs a quick "breakfast" from one of the vending machines. He spends most of his mornings yawning and complains that he cannot concentrate on his work. Joe feels that the way he looks on the job is not important. He tells you, "As long as I do my job, that's all that is necessary." What kind of impression do you think Joe is making on his supervisor? How do *you* feel about Joe's appearance?

Illus. 3–1. Good Grooming: That Clean and Shining Look

You have probably had the experience of taking an examination after you sat up all night trying to cram the information into your head. You know how difficult it is to make decisions, to pay attention to detail, even to think when you are not in good physical condition. The same situation occurs when you are on the job. Your physical fitness contributes to your job success. Physical exercise, enough sleep, the right foods, the right weight—all of these contribute to your success.

Having good health is a great advantage as you move into the mainstream of employment. Unfortunately, we do not always appreciate this fact. It may be that you will not value your good health as you should until it is in danger of slipping away.

How *do* you feel? Do you have colds and flu every winter? Do you get headaches frequently? Do you feel weak and dizzy at 10 in the morning and 4 in the afternoon? How about your endurance? Can you stand up under long hikes? Do you play tennis? Do you swim? It may be that *you* do these things, but far too many young adults have, seemingly, never been out of a car in their lives! They ride to school; they ride to meetings; their parents drive them around their paper routes. It is to be expected that their muscle tone may leave something to be desired.

Whatever your present state of health, you should resolve at once to maintain it or, if need be, to improve it. Improving your health will be like opening a door to greater vitality and enjoyment of life, so do it gladly. It pays off in the long run.

Good Health Habits

First of all, good health is the result of good health habits. If you smoke too much, skip meals, take sleeping pills to go to sleep and pep pills to wake up, there can be only one ultimate conclusion: Your health will break down. Of course, the opposite is true. To build up your health, you must develop and maintain the kind of health habits that increase your general well-being.

Think Thin!

The recent growth of reducing salons, weight-watching organizations, and books on dieting points up a serious health problem in our present affluent society. Many of us eat too much of the wrong foods. Obesity, or being overweight, is perhaps not really a barrier to success in some occupations. But in others it can be a definite problem. It is a hard one to solve, moreover, because many overweight individuals do not realize they eat too much. They are hardly conscious that they *are* eating, as a matter of fact. Certain experiments have shown that, instead of responding to hunger as a normal person does, the overweight individual responds to other cues: hot-dog stands, smells of cooking, commercials on television, a bowl of potato chips, a candy store. This person actually makes a habit of eating when seeing, smelling, hearing, or reading about food.

If you are a few pounds over your normal weight, you are lucky. It is fairly easy to lose up to ten pounds by drinking lots of water, by eating only high-protein foods, by cutting each meal in half, and by refraining from between-meal snacks. Any of these methods will do the trick. If you are 20 or more pounds above what you should be, however, you should see a doctor. Get the doctor's O.K. for a schedule of diet and exercise. And stick with it. You will be better looking and happier. Most important of all, you will add years to your life.

Stand Up Straight!

One of the most obvious and most easily corrected health problems is poor posture. Developing good posture is really a matter of habit. You can work at this habit anytime, anywhere. It is not necessary to invest in expensive equipment for practicing good posture. Nor is it essential to set aside 15 minutes a day for such practice. All you have to do is say to yourself, several times an *hour*, "Stand tall," "Sit tall,"—and then do it!

Good posture does not mean throwing your shoulders back; it means stretching your ears upward. Imagine you are trying to reach the ceiling with your ears. This is the way to start. Just reach up with those ears and the rest of your body will automatically follow suit. You will find yourself slumping now and then, of course. But back you will go into good posture if you remember to stand tall, to reach upward.

The second part of good posture is *abdomen in*. This can be practiced while walking, standing, or sitting; and it takes a good bit of practice to develop a strong muscle tone that keeps a flat abdomen all the time. Just keep practicing. After you have learned to stand tall, it will be much easier to keep your abdomen pulled in.

Another part of good posture is good walking position. Feet should be pointed straight ahead—not pointed out and not pointed in. If you walk in this manner, stretching tall, your arms will fall naturally at your sides; and you will probably realize another dividend, better relaxation. Many of us are tense partly because we stand or sit in a tense "shoulders-up" position. Remember, the shoulders should not stretch up—just the ears.

Fun and Games

Another part of good health is recreation. Every young adult—and older ones, too—should have some plain fun now and then. The choice, however, must be left to each individual. Do you like organized sports? If you do, your problem will be

Illus. 3–2. Remember the benefits of recreation.

Photo Courtesy of PepsiCo, Inc.

solved quickly. Bowling, golf, tennis, basketball, football, baseball, hiking, swimming, skiing—the list goes on and on. If you like sports, see that you play your favorite game at least once a week, and more often if you can spare the time.

What if you don't like sports? The important point is that participation is the key to recreation. You do not get the same benefit from merely watching a basketball game on television. You must be active in the game or sport if you are to get the greatest benefit from it.

The healthiest people are involved in something they *enjoy.* So—get involved. Are you stagestruck but lacking in acting experience? Then volunteer to help paint scenery, sell tickets, sweep out the stage. Would you like to write on the school paper but have no background in this sort of work? Then offer to sell advertising, act as a reporter, or type other people's stories. Participation is the great advantage that comes from working in extracurricular activities. There is always room for someone who is willing to work and who will start at the bottom. If your recreation is relatively sedentary, however, you must get your exercise in some other way. Walking or jogging is excellent exercise. Another method of exercise available to all is calisthenics. Even five minutes a day, done regularly and with vigor, will do wonders for you.

You Are What You Eat

You probably know what you should eat; but do you? Are you one of the skip-breakfast, grab-a-donut-at-ten, skip-lunch, have-a-candy-bar-at-four kind of people? If so, now is the time to reform. You cannot function at your best without good food.

At the risk of repeating what you have heard many times before, an adequate diet includes protein (meat, fish, eggs, milk), whole grain cereals, and fresh fruits and vegetables every day. You don't need as many starches as many of us eat. Most of us eat too many sweets. The quickest way to get into a vicious circle, by the way, is to overeat sweets. The carbohydrate habit can be broken, however, mainly by making sure that your diet is adequate in the whole grains that provide the B vitamins.

If you will try a balanced diet for one month, you will be convinced. Clear eyes, clear complexion, abundant energy—all of these will be natural by-products. Why not try it?

Do You Get Your Eight Hours?

Perhaps you don't get enough sleep. In these days of frantic overdoing, it is quite likely that the adage "Early to bed and early to rise" is seldom followed. But good sleep habits can be developed, just as can good eating habits. If you have formed the habit of staying up late—to watch the late-late show, let us say—you may find it impossible to get to sleep if you go to bed at 10:30.

The thing to do, is to taper off gradually. If midnight has been your retiring hour for quite some time, make it 11:45 for a week or two. After you have learned to go to sleep at 11:45, cut it back to 11:30, and so on until you can go to sleep in time to get seven to eight hours of sleep a night.

While you are working on this project, you may find that taking "catnaps" of ten minutes now and then through the day helps you to get the rest that you need. Even if you do not go to sleep, relaxing completely in an easy chair for ten minutes or so will soon become a most refreshing pause.

Appropriate Dress

If you were cast in a school or community play as a successful young worker in the firm of your choice, how would you dress? First impressions are often lasting ones, and just as often they are made on the basis of your appearance. Your friends may judge you or excuse you on the basis of your kind heart or your past actions, but none of this information is available to people when they first meet you. They can judge you only on what they see. They may actually make decisions about your personality and capability on the basis of that first impression. You can make that first impression work for you if you dress the part.

It has been said repeatedly that you can't legislate morality. It seems that the past decade has taught us that you can't legislate fashion, either. The day is apparently over when Paris or Savile Row turns American buyers into obedient sheep. All people develop minds of their own in the matter of what they should wear. Of course, the fashion designers are still trying.

Since the authors do not have a crystal ball handy, no attempt will be made to predict what the future will bring. It seems that the day has come when we can wear almost anything. But some employers, even in this modern day, do not see it that way. To be on the safe side, then, you should imagine some happy medium between complete freedom to wear whatever you wish and the strict dress code which was enforced in business not long ago. Just remember that the world of business is more conservative than schools, colleges, the entertainment world, or the world of sports.

First, before you apply for the job you want, visit that company. Observe the secretaries, the head of the sales department, the vice-presidents. You will find that the higher up the ladder of success these workers have climbed, the more "businesslike" their clothing and general appearance has become. Second, after you have taken the job you want, don't be the leader in taking up the newest fad. For one thing, fads are expensive because they don't last long. The main reason for letting others be the first to adopt the newest fashion, however, is that the

Illus. 3–3. Project a well-groomed image.

fashion leader will be criticized by the more conservative executives in the organization. As a beginner, you can't afford that criticism. When the new fashion is fully accepted, you may safely join in. Until you are secure in your job, however, you shouldn't take chances.

Good Grooming: That Clean and Shining Look

Whether you are in high school, in college, or have reached that "over thirty" level, you cannot be a success in the world of work if you persist in defying the rules of good grooming. This applies to the business office, the grocery store, the restaurant, the warehouse—as long as your work brings you into contact with other people.

Free expression is fine. But, for the business person, free expression in dress and grooming must be done in leisure time. Business, in order to exist and continue to hire workers, must project an image of dependability, of solidity, of trust. Those managers and owners who do the hiring of beginning workers believe that such an image is destroyed if the employees of the business firm present a picture of unkempt carelessness.

Body Odor

Nothing makes one less popular either in an employment situation or in society than unpleasant odors. It is a fact of life, however, that we may be all too aware of the problem in others, but unaware that we, too, may be at fault. A daily shower or bath plus the use of a deodorant is usually adequate for safety; however, if special body odors are a problem, you should consult a doctor. Also, in this matter, you must be your own detective; truly, your best friend won't tell you. Sometimes just more frequent bathing is all that is required.

Clean Clothing

Occasionally the problem is not body cleanliness but the habit of wearing a shirt or a blouse longer than one should. If you are in business, a shirt should probably be worn only one day before it is laundered. Cottons and other washable fabrics may also need washing after each wearing. Woolens and knits should be sent to the cleaners frequently, perhaps after three wearings; these wearings should be separated by several days of airing, however.

Before putting away clothing that has been worn, expose it to fresh air. An outdoor clothesline is ideal for periodic airing. If this isn't possible, however, let clothing worn during the day air elsewhere.

A Clean Body

Everyone is aware that soiled hands should be washed immediately. Fingernails must always be clean if you are in the public eye. If you work with duplicating machines, or if your hands become smudged from carbon paper, special creams and liquids will remove all but the most stubborn stains.

Hair must always be clean, and this means frequent shampoos. Dandruff should be controlled by daily brushing and by the use of special shampoos. If you have special problems with your hair, such as excessive oiliness, dryness, or dandruff, it may be wise to consult a dermatologist.

Skin Care

Nothing contributes so much to an attractive appearance as healthy, glowing skin. Such a state of affairs involves more than health. The avoidance of certain rich foods is necessary in many cases. Plenty of fresh fruits, exercise, vitamins—all of these will affect your skin—plus sufficient rest. In addition to these factors there is cleanliness. Your skin must be clean! This means the removal of all makeup and grime before retiring. It means soap-and-water cleansing in some cases and cleansing cream plus astringents in others. Whatever your skin type, you should never permit an oily, smudged look. If your skin is oily, eliminate most fats from your diet and wash your face with special soaps several times a day. Follow each washing with the use of an astringent.

If ordinary cleanliness, diet, and rest do not care adequately for your skin, consult a dermatologist. The time and money invested in such professional help will be worth it to you in improved appearance and freedom from worry. If you have acne, the help of a dermatologist is absolutely essential. Today even scars resulting from bad cases of acne can be helped.

If you possess a clear and attractive skin, count your blessings. Then start a regimen that will keep your skin attractive. The same rules should be followed: adequate rest, sensible diet, perfect cleanliness, and exercise. One word of caution must be given: never squeeze a blemish that appears on your face. Wash your face carefully and cover the offending blemish with a medicated ointment. It will take care of itself in a short time, but any tampering with it may result in disaster.

Hair Care

The importance of keeping your hair clean and shining has already been discussed. No matter how beautiful the curl, how luxuriant the growth, or how modish the style, you cannot have attractive hair unless it is clean. One successful buyer in a large shop said, "If your hair is clean, your face looks cleaner." The hair does create an illusion either of cleanliness or untidiness.

An old and tested way to care for the hair is to brush it one hundred strokes a day. At first, such brushing may make the hair oilier, and more frequent shampoos will be required. After a few weeks, however, you will notice a new shine to your hair, a cleaner look than you had before. Such brushing also improves the health of the scalp. Every day or so it is helpful to wash your brush and comb; a bit of ammonia in the water will make the task quick and easy. A clean brush and comb will help to keep your hair clean as it is brushed.

Hair styles have changed radically in the past few years, and they may change even more radically in the future. It is a good plan, nonetheless, to avoid extremes. Whatever the style, hair should be clean and smooth. The degree of oiliness in the hair should be the deciding factor as to frequency of shampooing. Hair dressings should not interfere with a natural look.

Just as good points can be accentuated and bad points minimized by careful clothing selection, so can your hair style flatter your face, give an appearance of height, or call attention to your least attractive feature. It is advisable to consult a good hairdresser as to the most becoming hair style because hair arrangement can give illusions that change the shape of your face and that minimize or magnify either good or bad features. The way you wear your hair can also make you look taller or shorter. With the general features of a becoming style in mind, you can modify the hair style that is in fashion to suit you. It is unwise to go on wearing a favorite hair style long after it has passed into the out-of-date category.

Test for Good Grooming

To simplify the grooming process, it may be helpful if one has some sort of yardstick to measure the extent to which it has been achieved. Just how well groomed should a person in business be?

Tests for Good Grooming

If you are planning to enter the business world, you should take the problem of grooming seriously. In some kinds of work, to be sure, the problem is not so crucial. In business, however, everyone you meet will be judging you and your firm by your appearance. Your co-workers, too, will be affected by the care you take with grooming yourself. Each day you should mentally check off the following:

A person is well groomed when

1) Body and teeth are clean and free from odor
2) Skin is clear, not oily
3) Hair is neatly trimmed, clean, and combed
4) Hands have a cared-for look
5) Shoes are shined
6) Socks or hose are clean and not allowed to wrinkle around the ankles
7) Clothes are fresh, pressed, with no spots
8) Clothes are appropriate for business and fit properly

The Habit of Personal Neatness

Neatness and grooming are important, not only because they indicate orderliness and good taste, but also because of the feeling they give you. If you picture yourself and feel that others picture you as an example of a poised, well-groomed business person, you will find it easier to play that role. The self-confidence that comes from feeling that your appearance is right makes it easier to give your entire attention to the tasks before you.

> Janet, sent to interview for a prospective job, reports a successful termination to the interview. She is told that she was chosen from many applicants because she displayed traits which the company felt were important. Janet had taken special care to dress neatly for the interview. Her new employer told her, "There were other applicants who were more educationally prepared for the job than you, but because of the impression of neatness you gave me at the interview, I selected you."

Questions and Projects

1. Suppose you have been hired to work as a dental technician. You must wear plain white uniforms for work, but they may be of any material you prefer. Investigate the cost, upkeep, and wearing qualities of three different fabrics commonly used for such uniforms. Which one would you choose? Why?

2. Jeff has just taken a position as a typist in a small office. The ventilation is inadequate and there is no air conditioning. Jeff's supervisor, Ms. Christensen, has a desk very close to Jeff's. On a particularly hot day, Ms. Christensen has the janitor move his desk into another corner some distance away. Should Jeff consider this a reflection on his grooming? If you were Jeff, would you say anything to Ms. Christensen? If so, what would you say?

3. Do you think a person's weight has any effect on grooming requirements? If you were your present height and 30 pounds heavier, what additional grooming precautions would you need to take?

4. From your own experience, can you think of an application of the importance of neatness? Write the situation down and use it for class discussion.

5. You are the only woman working in the data processing division of a large firm. All of the men in your division wear white shirts but remove their coats during working hours. What type of clothing would you buy to wear to work?

6. Do you exercise regularly? If you do, draw up a schedule showing the amount and the kinds of exercise you have had in the last two weeks. What plans have you for following a regular schedule of time for exercise?

7. It has been said that "your best friend won't tell you" that you are troubled with body odor. To whom can you appeal if you honestly want to know?

8. If you have not yet begun your career in the business world, what changes in your present wardrobe will you make when you go to work?

9. Make a list of the groups in your community that offer opportunities for regular exercise. Find out the benefits of each group you are eligible to join, the membership dues, the obligations, and other information.

10. What will you wear when you are interviewed by a prospective employer?

11. What preparations for your appearance will you make the evening before an employment interview?

12. Make a checklist of duties that should be performed regularly in order to maintain a neat, clean wardrobe.

13. Chris wears shirts two days before laundering them. Dale questions this practice, but Chris says there are not enough shirts in the closet to wear a clean one each day. Is there a better solution than the one Chris uses?

14. Robin is employed in an insurance firm. Robin's supervisor suggests that Robin choose more conservative clothes for the office. Robin later tells you that clothing is a personal matter and that the supervisor was wrong to make such a suggestion. What would you tell Robin? Should Robin be concerned about the supervisor's suggestion?

Case Problems

1. "Moonlighting."

Ray Benton works as a junior accountant in the accounting department of a large firm. Ray is ambitious and particularly anxious to make more money than his salary as a beginner pays him. To add to his salary, he keeps books for a number of small firms, doing the work at night and on weekends. He also makes out income tax returns for several of these companies and the individuals working in them. Because he wants to keep up with his field, he reads the accounting periodicals at night before going to sleep.

All this activity naturally interferes with his rest. Also, he has not taken a vacation in three years, preferring to catch up on his outside work during this period. There is an opening for a senior accountant in the firm, and Ray is being considered for the position. Miss Henry, the controller, has noted Ray's tenseness, his look of fatigue, and his apparent lack of interest in his work. She asks one of Ray's friends if he knows of anything that could be wrong. The friend tells Miss Henry that Ray is overworking. Unable to understand how this could be so (as Ray's work load in the company is only average), Miss Henry calls Ray in and asks him what work he is doing. Ray tells her that he wants to make more money and what he is doing to earn it. What would you do if you were Miss Henry?

2. Samples From the Stock Room.

Jim Thurman worked for the shipping department of Hogles Company. He hoped to become a sales representative for the firm someday. After two years, however, he was neither given a raise nor promoted while co-workers were transferred to the retail sales department. Finally, Jim became discouraged and decided to quit. Before he left, he asked his employer why he had never been promoted. The answer was that when Jim reported to work his hair was not neatly combed, his shoes were not polished, his clothes were not pressed, and his nails were not clean. Jim left feeling that his employer should have told him previously that his appearance was not measuring up to the firm's standards. Yet he could not see why it should have been necessary for him to be neat in the shipping room.

1. Do you think Jim was right in thinking that neatness did not matter in the shipping room?
2. Do you feel Jim's employer should have mentioned Jim's lack of neatness when it was first noted?
3. Do you think that the quality of a person's work can be predicted from personal grooming?

3. Your Best Friend Won't Tell You.

Peggy works in a word processing unit. One day four of the other employees whose desks were near Peggy's made an appointment to talk with the supervisor, Mrs. Washington. When the meeting was held, Peggy's co-workers told the supervisor they would all like to have their desks moved away from Peggy. When asked their reason, they said they couldn't stand Peggy's disagreeable body odor. Mrs. Washington thanked them and promised to do something about the problem.

1. Assuming you are the supervisor, how would you handle this prob-
    lem?
    a. Would you tell Peggy that her co-workers had complained? Why
        or why not?
    b. Would you begin your conversation with Peggy with a question
        or with a statement?
2. Discuss the matter with four of your classmates. After you have
    agreed on a solution, write the exact words you think you would
    say to Peggy.
3. As an alternative to writing the supervisor's conversation with Peggy,
    perform your version of the solution to this problem as a role-playing
    assignment.

4.   Constructive Criticism.

Bob McAfee was the bookkeeper for the Worth Mercantile Company. As he was working he would often run his hands through his
hair, leaving it mussed and untidy. Bob's desk could be seen through
a window by the customers as they came into the notions department.
The head of this department, Mr. Cameron, although not connected
directly with the bookkeeping department, spoke to Bob about his
habit and told him how untidy it looked through the window. Bob replied,
"I've had the habit for years. I do it without thinking when I'm working."

1. Was Mr. Cameron justified in criticizing a worker in another depart-
    ment?
2. Should Bob have paid any attention to Mr. Cameron, since he was
    in a different department?
3. How would you have reacted to this criticism if you had been Bob?
4. Mr. Cameron might have gone to Bob's superior with his criticism.
    Would this have been preferable? Why or why not?

5.   Wisdom in Spending.

Emi Kimura is fortunate in obtaining summer employment in a
bank. There is a possibility that if she does well, she may obtain permanent work later in the same office. The other employees dress better
than Emi does, and they spend more money for recreation and entertainment. Emi has been trying to save for further study but wonders
if she should not spend more on her clothes to impress her employer
favorably so that she may be considered for a permanent position.

1. If Emi decides to spend all or most of her money now, how will
    she benefit?
2. If she decides to save her money, how will she benefit?
3. What would you do in this case? Why?

Chapter 4
Your standards of conduct

Pat and Jan were sharing a hero sandwich at the deli where they often meet for lunch. "I'm amazed at what some people get away with in the hardware business," said Jan. "If you want to, you can get away with anything." "It's the same at our bank. But you could find yourself unemployed—maybe in jail," Pat responded. "I'm not talking about crime," Jan said, "I mean things like writing letters on company time. And using the postage meter for personal mail. Taking extra time at the water cooler. Showing favoritism to customers who bribe you with Christmas gifts. Not reporting cash transactions to avoid income tax. I could go on and on—and they get away with it!" There was a pause. Then Pat said, "You know, Jan, we don't *have* to pay for this sandwich. Or do we?"

When you take your first job, you will be working with a cross section of people. Some will have an "anything goes" standard of conduct; others will be strict in their views of what should and should not be done. It will be up to you to set moral standards for yourself. Whatever they are, think them through; decide for yourself; then stick with them. Your morality will mean conformity to the standards of what you believe is right.

Illus. 4–1.   Your Reputation: Dedicated and Conscientious

Your Reputation: A Valuable Asset

Many people are concerned by a lack of ethics and morality in business. Because business is concerned with profits, because it is competitive, and because success is based on rivalry, some will argue that business cannot be moral.

An ambitious business person, however, must look beyond the surface evidence and study the long-range results of morality in business. This survey will reveal that companies that have become firmly established through years of service are more interested in protecting their good reputation than in making a single sale or in making quick profits. Young firms, too, who want to establish lasting goodwill are more interested in their integrity than in the profit of the moment. In testing the effect of morality, take a hard look at the businesses that have successfully stood the test of time.

As a business person you should guard your record of morality because it is a valuable possession. You should guard it because you are ethical, have faith, and because you have a sense of fair play and a social conscience. You should guard it for selfish reasons, too, because it is as valuable to you in business as capital or education.

Successful business people should also be interested, not in a moment of glory and success, but in long-range respect. Seldom are there any secrets in business. Even long after an incident of immorality, someone will remember. Facts can come to light in other ways, too, for there are many types of records. That a person did not make a sale, that a task was poorly completed, that an employee was promoted will probably be forgotten. But immorality will become a part of the record. If this record is not in writing, it will be whispered.

On many details of morality people do not agree, but some basic principles are common to the consciences of all people. Other basic principles, in addition to those of all society, are recognized by business people.

Success-related personality factors, as indicated earlier, are dedication, loyalty, honesty, and conscientiousness. These personal qualities are highly prized by employers. Therefore, your success in the world of work depends on the impression your employers have about your standards of conduct.

Just as a business firm has its "image" to develop and protect, so you must develop and protect your personal image. The following sections will focus on some of the typical situations in which you may build up or tear down that image. You will see that there are many opportunities to build up or tear down—many choices to make. These choices will challenge your integrity and strength of character. Sometimes there is a high price to pay when you live up to your own standards of conduct. But after you have developed a reputation for being dedicated, loyal, honest and conscientious, that reputation will pay off. Doors of opportunity will open for you. Employers will give you preference in hiring. They will reward you with advancement and greater responsibility. On the other hand, if you should develop a reputation for being less than conscientious, inclined to dishonesty, or lacking in loyalty, doors of opportunity will remain closed. You should expect employers to take this image into consideration. Advancement and increased responsibility will pass you by. In the long run, a bad reputation can be a heavy burden to carry.

The Many Faces of Dishonesty

Seldom, if ever, can you expect to find a totally honest person. Employers do not expect that. They do not expect absolute dedication, loyalty or conscientious effort under all conditions. Therefore, when a supervisor writes a letter of recommendation saying, "Lou is an honest person," the message is that Lou, in comparison with other workers, is more honest than most. Under extreme stress almost anyone may be expected to behave with less than absolute honesty. But the person with high standards of honesty will be able to resist great pressure and remain honest. Your challenge is to set standards of honesty for yourself which will cause your employers to admire and respect you—to expect what they consider to be a satisfactory level of honesty in your dealings with them.

Rather than present a list of rules for honesty in employment, some situations will be presented which might challenge your own honesty. As the possible alternatives to the situation are discussed, you will begin to understand what honesty means in the world of work. Rather than simply trying to set standards of honesty for you , this will help you see what typical employers might expect of employees with reputations for being honest. Then you should be able to measure your own personal standards against those of your future employers. Hopefully you will want to set high standards of honesty for yourself. In the long run, your honesty will be rewarded.

Larceny

Larceny, by definition, means to take something fully intending *not* to return the thing to its owner. Larceny is theft and a larcenist is a thief. But any judge will tell you that many convicted larcenists do not think of themselves as criminals. For example, you may know someone who has taken merchandise from a store without paying for it. But do you think of your acquaintances who have been guilty of shoplifting as criminals? (Yes, larceny is, legally, a criminal offense.)

There are many kinds of larceny in the workplace. *Grand larceny* is the legal term for stealing something of great value (over a legally specified amount). *Petty larceny* describes the theft of something of little value. The legal penalties are greater for grand larceny, but petty larceny is probably a greater problem for employers. Shoplifting of merchandise by the employees in a retail business is only one form of the problem, however. Employee theft of supplies, equipment, and materials is another form of petty theft which causes employers great concern.

Most business owners and managers will say privately that they expect some petty theft by employees, just as retailers expect a certain amount of shoplifting to occur. But not all employers use the same strategies for eliminating employee theft. A few assume that they can make the consequences so harsh that no one will dare to steal anything. They may press legal charges in court, possibly spending far more money than the cost of the stolen items. This helps to dramatize and publicize the fact that the management considers petty theft to be a serious offense. More often, however, the offender will be fired on the spot. The employer may assume that the damage to the employee's reputation is punishment enough. And, indeed, it may be.

Suppose, for a moment, you had been convicted of petty theft. Think of how you might feel as you face an employment interviewer. How can you soften the effect of the petty larceny

Illus. 4–2. Maintain your reputation for honesty in spite of temptation.

Courtesy of Data Terminal Systems

conviction on your employment record? On the positive side, think of how you might feel having a spotless employment record, knowing your previous employer has, in a letter of recommendation, described you as a completely honest person—one who can be trusted. You have never been known to take anything, not even a postage stamp or a paper clip, for personal use.

Knowing what is acceptable behavior and what is not, as your employer sees it, is not always easy. Following are some examples of behavior that some employers may allow. Others may consider such behavior to be dishonest.

Taking small quantities of inexpensive office supplies such as pencils, file folders, and transparent tape.

Sending personal mail on company stationery, using company postage, and using company long-distance telephone lines for personal calls.

Taking supplies or materials that the company produces or uses in large quantities.

Taking things that the employer has no use for and wants to dispose of. Some examples are day-old bakery goods, used packing boxes, surplus or waste building materials, defective or damaged merchandise, scrap paper, and free samples of merchandise or supplies.

What you must do to protect your reputation for honesty is find out what your employer's expectations are and be sure your standards of conduct conform to those expectations. You can learn about what is expected by simply asking, "Terry, do you mind if I take a pickup truck load of sand to fill the sandbox I made for my cousin?" Or you might be less direct, "Dana, may I use the company long-distance line to call my parents in Minneapolis, or should I have the call billed to my home phone?"

You may also learn what is acceptable and what is not by observing and talking with your co-workers. But be careful. You may find yourself—along with others—violating your employer's rules. An example of this occurred in a large construction firm in a western state. Jane noticed several of her co-workers taking company-supplied flashlight batteries in their lunch pails. When she asked if she could take some for her own use, a veteran worker replied, "Sure, we take a few batteries for deer hunting every year. Help yourself." Jane took six batteries, three in each coat pocket. The office manager happened to notice the bulging pockets. Jane's explanation that, "Everyone else is doing it and they told me it was OK," was not very convincing. Fortunately, Jane was only reprimanded. But company officials investigated and found a *200 percent increase* in the use of flashlight batteries— always just before deer hunting season.

Expense Account Abuse

Many business occupations involve travel, meals, and lodging at company expense. Selling "on the road," travel to deliver merchandise or to service customers' equipment, and to participate in business conferences are cases in point. Some companies have liberal expense accounting policies. They trust the employee to keep personal records and simply report what was spent. Other employers enforce elaborate rules and regulations with lots of paperwork. These detailed rules and recordkeeping procedures are designed to protect the employer from employees who might use the expense accounting system to obtain extra income. Here are some examples of petty theft by using expense account "loopholes."

Reporting more expensive meals than actually eaten.

Asking reimbursement for meals not paid for (such as those received on an airplane).

Including liquor (reported as food) on expense accounts.

Reporting greater automobile mileage than actually driven.

Riding the bus but reporting taxi fares.

Two people sharing a ride and both asking for full reimbursement.

Staying in exclusive hotels, traveling first-class, or eating at the most expensive restaurants.

Asking reimbursement for expenses for vacation time (taking an extra day for recreation at the end of a business trip).

Including personal long-distance telephone calls on a hotel bill.

Some of these practices are clearly dishonest and unacceptable. Some appear to be questionable. Others may seem, to most people, to be perfectly acceptable. Your challenge, as always, is to learn what your employer expects of you in a given situation. Then you must avoid abuses that can damage your reputation for honesty.

As an inexperienced worker, you will need to make a special effort to learn "how the game is played." But be aware that you may encounter individuals who will set a bad example— "bending the rules" or cheating whenever and however they can. At the opposite extreme you will find individuals who live by very high moral standards. For instance, they may stay with friends or relatives and pass the savings in hotel bills along to the employer. Or they may take advantage of the lowest possible air fare and travel at an inconvenient time to get a lower-priced ticket. They may eat inexpensive meals, carry bag lunches, and in other ways conserve on food expenses. In one unusual case, a sales representative was found to be reporting unusually low travel expenses. When the expense account auditor investigated, it was found that the representative owned a small car which used very little gasoline. Making sure the reimbursement only covered *actual* expenses, the representative was reporting less than the actual mileage.

When you find someone behaving this way, chances are it will be the boss. The owner or manager of a business knows that lower expenses mean higher profits. When *you* get the profits, your motivation to economize is increased. But you should realize that in the long run both you and your employer will benefit when you help your employer make a profit. And just as there are people who use the expense account to steal from their employers, there are people who use it to conserve and reduce expenses for their employers. Probably you will find most of your co-workers' actions to be somewhere between these extremes. The majority of people are honest in reporting their actual expenses; they lose or gain very little.

To conclude this discussion of expense accounts, consider this: When employees' personal standards of honesty are high, a relaxed, trusting relationship grows. Employers seldom question or even review the expense accounts reported by trusted employees. When necessary, the employees can report unusually high expenses without hesitation. It is a pleasure to work in such an atmosphere. But it is far from pleasant to work in an atmosphere of insecurity and mistrust that results when employers see expense accounting as a potential tool for petty larceny by their employees.

Perquisites

A perquisite is defined as "a privilege, gain or profit incidental to regular salary or wages; especially one expected or promised." As this definition shows, there are many perquisites that have nothing to do with a person's moral standards. For example, Norman works at a restaurant. He gets an hourly wage plus tips. He also gets free meals for himself and a 50 percent discount on food he or anyone in his family buys.

But for every perquisite there is usually an opportunity for some kind of abuse. In our example, Norman may decide to have a party. His employer probably would be upset to see that Norman used his food discount privilege to buy forty dollars worth of fried chicken for twenty dollars. Or Norman may get into a habit of ordering the most expensive steak sandwich just at closing time and taking most of it home supposedly for his dog—or worse—leaving it on his plate.

Another challenge to Norman's integrity is how he manages his tips. He may occasionally pick up tips intended for a co-worker. He may hold some money back for himself when tips are to be shared with other employees. He may record only part of his tips to avoid paying income tax on the unreported earnings.

Almost any job you can think of has certain perquisites, and almost every perquisite offers some opportunity for exploitation—or dishonesty. Consider the following situations.

Many retail stores offer employee discounts on merchandise.

Employees of a small midwestern meat-packing plant (including office workers) may buy veal tenderloin at one-third of the market price.

Employees of a large automotive service station are allowed to take any parts that may be discarded when repairs are made.

Many automobile and motorcycle dealers allow their employees to drive used vehicles that are in stock. (Some dealers allow employees to drive customers' vehicles!)

An office machines company gives high school business teachers first choice in the purchase of typewriters that have been traded in—for a small fraction of the market value.

A television dealer allows service department employees to work on their own sets, evenings and weekends, with parts provided at the dealer's cost.

These are only a few examples. You probably could think of many more. Also, you could probably imagine many different ways to take advantage of such situations, to an employer's disadvantage. This is where your good judgment, your sense of fair play, and your basic honesty will guide you.

Bribery

When you first think of "bribery" as a form of employee dishonesty, you will probably be reminded of gambling, political pressure, and "white collar crime" involving business executives. But bribery, on a small scale, may occur at any level in a business enterprise.

Here is a different example of a form of bribery that you may encounter. Lee, a salesclerk in a pharmacy, often chooses the brand of a product for the customer. In this instance four brands of cold medicine, all having the same formula, were on display. Whenever a customer asked for cold medicine without specifying a brand, the salesclerks would make the choice themselves. One drug wholesaler found a way to encourage salesclerks to give preference to Brand X when selecting cold medicine for a customer.

This is how the scheme worked. A removable sticker, about the size of a postage stamp, was placed on every package of Brand X. When the drug firm representative made regular visits to a pharmacy, all the stickers each salesclerk had collected would be redeemed at fifteen cents each. Lee was able to earn about fifteen dollars in cash per week this way over and above regular wages. The drug wholesaler did not refer to the payoff money as bribery, however. A more socially acceptable name was needed for it. So the wholesaler chose to refer to the small bribes as "perquisites" and every salesclerk was given a little box with the word "perks" printed on it.

Of course, being in a position to benefit from petty bribery *is* a perquisite if you take advantage of it. And many people would not consider it wrong for a salesclerk to accept the "perks" described above. Eventually, in court, a Brand X competitor was able to show that the scheme was illegal. Only the Brand X drug wholesaler was punished. But were the salespeople partly at fault? Were the pharmacy managers at fault when they permitted the petty bribery to occur? Does the fact that some stores did not allow their employees to accept the "perks" affect your opinion?

Perquisites are more often associated with high level executive positions. Some examples are reserved parking space, country club memberships, stock purchase options, and the use of company cars. One linen supply company executive arranged for the company to provide *two* cars. One was used for travel on company business. The other was supposed to be used by the maintenance supervisor. However, all the maintenance workers were employed at one plant. Because the maintenance supervisor never used the car, the executive's children used it, choosing a new car every year at company expense.

These cases illustrate how petty bribery and the abuse of special privileges can occur in the world of work. Following are a few other examples. In each instance you will see the same pattern: (a) The employee is in a position to control something of value. (b) Someone who wants to benefit through favored treatment is willing to pay. (c) A deal is made. Here are the examples:

(a) Gordon collects tickets at a movie theater.
(b) Phil, Sue, and Mary Ann go to a movie. Gordon accepts two tickets for three people.
(c) After the show, Gordon joins Mary Ann to make it a double date.

(a) The purchasing manager has responsibility for obtaining supplies for the hospital.
(b) The surgical supplies salesperson wants to sell bandages to the hospital.
(c) On Saturday the purchasing manager and the surgical supplies salesperson play two rounds of golf (paid for on the salesperson's expense account). On Monday the hospital places an order with the surgical supplies salesperson.

(a) The receptionist schedules appointments with the executive. (Appointments with the executive are valuable.)
(b) The client (a seafood wholesaler) is willing to pay the receptionist for scheduling appointments for her ahead of other clients.
(c) At Christmastime the client gives the receptionist fifteen pounds of frozen lobster—as a present. (Actually, both individuals understand that the lobster is given in return for favoritism in scheduling appointments with the executive. There is no written or spoken contract. But a deal *is* made.)

(a) The store display specialist has construction skills and materials available to her. (Also, she *loves* lobster.)
(b) The receptionist wants a planter for her office. (She has fifteen pounds of frozen lobster.)
(c) The display specialist builds a planter for the receptionist's office using company time and materials. She gets fifteen pounds of frozen lobster—as a gift.

As you can see from these examples, petty bribery is a common practice. It takes many forms. Sometimes it is not really obviously unethical or immoral. But you may find yourself in situations where you have opportunities to participate in petty bribery schemes that you know are wrong. Again, set high standards of ethical behavior for yourself.

The Dedicated Worker

Thus far in this chapter you have explored what it means to develop your reputation for honesty. Now consider what it means for your reputation to be dedicated, loyal, and conscientious.

Just as honesty is a personality trait that shapes your behavior when you are tempted to be dishonest, dedication is also a part of your personality. A dedicated employee is likely to exhibit several positive attitudes, including loyalty and being conscientious. Your dedication will show in your standard of conduct when you face such opportunities (and temptations) as the following:

> to do your own thing on company time;
>
> to put down co-workers as you climb the ladder of success;
>
> to gossip about your employer;
>
> to get even when you feel mistreated by your employer;
>
> to keep quiet when you know customers or co-workers are taking advantage of your employer;
>
> to allow social conversations with co-workers to interfere with getting the job done;
>
> to allow the use of alcohol or drugs to influence your job performance.

Being Conscientious

Earlier it was pointed out that many personality traits are sometimes evaluated differently by different people. What is conscientious behavior to one employer may appear to be pure laziness to another. So remember to learn your employer's expectations and be conscientious enough to build a good reputation. Learning how to be a conscientious worker is so important that Chapters 6, 7, and 8 are devoted to this topic. The purpose here is to point out some of the problems you will encounter.

In some work situations it seems that employees spend more energy and creativity figuring out ways to avoid work than they spend actually working. This seems to be a problem whenever several young people are working together without close supervision. It also occurs more often when people are involved in dull, routine work. But older workers and even executives can be found to play such games. Here are a few examples.

> Waiting ten minutes for someone to help you proofread two pages of typed material.
>
> Delivering a package that could be mailed instead.
>
> Going to someone's office for a conversation instead of using the telephone.
>
> Early starts and late stops for coffee breaks and lunch periods.

Carrying on social conversations (on the phone or in person) during working hours.

Doing your personal work (without anyone else knowing about it) during working hours.

Working fast (and carelessly) so there will be time, after all the work is done, to read, sleep, play cards, etc.

Working slowly—to make the work fill up the time available for it.

Daydreaming when you should be concentrating.

Causing a situation that will bring the work to a halt (a broken machine, shortage of materials, etc.).

Performing a task yourself when it could (and should) be done more efficiently by someone else.

Wasting time preparing for or talking about doing a job instead of getting to work and doing it.

Refusing to do something that you could do because "it is someone else's job."

Wasting a lot of time kidding around playing jokes or pranks on co-workers.

Pretending not to notice customers waiting to be served.

Some of the examples mentioned above may, at times, be normal and acceptable behavior. But any of them, when carried to the extreme, can cause your employer and co-workers to think of you as someone who wastes a lot of time. You probably have heard that "time is money." Most employers see it that way and they appreciate the worker who refuses to waste it.

In addition to conserving and using time well, the conscientious worker is not content with doing a mediocre—or average— job. Doing a *good* job without wasting time—that's what most employers will expect.

Loyalty

When you accept a job and an employer accepts you as a worker, a contract is made. You agree to work. The employer agrees to pay you for your work. But there is more to the contract. You expect to be allowed to learn and progress on the job. You expect good supervision and training. You expect the employer to be honest with you—and fair. You expect a reasonably safe, pleasant place to work. You expect to have occasional rest periods, time for lunch, extra pay for overtime work, and other fringe benefits.

Illus. 4–3. Demonstrate your dedication and loyalty to your employer.

The Ford Foundation

This is a very substantial list of expectations. But you are not entitled to any of them without meeting an equally substantial list of employer expectations. Many of those expectations are highlighted throughout this book—a positive attitude, productive work habits, initiative and motivation, knowledge and skills, and many more.

Among the most important of the typical employer's expectations is loyalty. Many employers complain that the young people of today are more likely to be disloyal than those of an earlier generation. This attitude is shown by some employers in their preference for hiring and promoting older workers. Of course, age and physical maturity do not automatically mean that the worker will be more mature in job performance and attitudes. But as a young worker, you will have to prove yourself. And your employer's *expectations* with respect to loyalty are most important.

Most employers are *very* intolerant of what they consider to be disloyal behavior. To help you understand what loyalty means to most employers, try to put yourself in the employer's position. Ask yourself, "How would I feel about this situation if I were the owner or manager of this business?"

Here is one example of how employee loyalty can be tested. Bill, as a waiter-trainee in a restaurant, noticed that some of the waiters and waitresses were receiving consistently larger tips than he was. Finally, he discovered the reason for it. Sandy, the person assigned to help train Bill, explained it this way. "What it amounts to is giving free drinks and salads," she said. "You refill soft drink glasses but forget to add the extra drinks to the check. You serve salads that were not ordered, and tell the customers that it is "on the house." Sometimes you just sort of forget to put drinks or salads on the check. Most often what they should have paid for the salads and drinks shows up in your tip."

Now, Bill found himself in a *dilemma*—a situation where one way or the other he was bound to create a problem for himself. Should he report this practice to his supervisor or should he go along with the scheme? As it turned out, Bill chose loyalty to the employer over loyalty to his dishonest co-workers. When Bill left his job to return to college, the manager expressed appreciation for his loyalty. Also, Bill was promised a job at any future time, and a good recommendation to any other prospective employer.

Sex, Drugs, and Alcohol Abuse

You may be the type of individual who lives by the highest standard of sexual morality and a person who never drinks alcohol or abuses drugs. If so, these standards of conduct will probably be an asset as you seek employment and advancement in the world of work. As with the other personality traits discussed in this chapter, employers have a variety of expectations. Basically, you will find employers having one of the following three points of view.

At one extreme is the employer who cares only about one thing—production. In this situation no one will be overly concerned about what you do when you are not on the job. Your private life is your own business, as far as your employer is concerned. Whatever you are privately, your employer will only be concerned with how well you do the job you were hired to do. You will be expected to keep your personal life and affairs in control so they have no effect on your work.

At the opposite extreme are employers who assume that anyone associated with the company must live by certain moral and personal behavior standards. Examples are when the person is employed by a church, local government, or a school or community organization that has a public image to protect. Such employers have been known to fire a person for having been seen walking out of a bar.

Between the two extremes described above are the employers who expect, like the first type of employer, that personal problems at home, drugs, and alcohol abuse will not influence job performance. But in addition, they may want to maintain a favorable company image. For example, a bank, a retail store, or a real estate agency might feel that their business would be hurt if customers think the company's salespeople are not of the highest moral character. This point of view is especially common in small communities (where company employees are recognized by everyone—and where stories of improper behavior get around quickly). Some of these employers may actually try to help their workers with company-sponsored programs. These programs may provide services such as counselors and doctors who can help with alcoholism and family problems.

In conclusion, remember that the higher your standards, the more options you have. You will have a wider selection of prospective employers. You will adapt and find acceptance in a greater variety of employment situations. You may find it difficult, at times, to maintain higher standards of conduct. But once you do, you will have good reason to take pride in yourself. Your chances for success and personal satisfaction will be increased. In the long run, *you* will be the winner.

Questions and Projects

1. You have heard it said that "honesty is the best policy." Yet we find many examples of successful business owners and managers who are accused of dishonesty—in advertising, selling methods, failing to stand behind what they sell, and so on. Is honesty the best policy in business today? In your opinion, why or why not?

2. As a class project, interview a variety of owners and managers of local companies. Ask them to give examples from their experiences of employee dishonesty. Also, ask what actions they usually take when they discover dishonest behavior.

3. Ask a law enforcement officer, an attorney, or a judge to talk to your class about petty larceny and "white collar crime" in the world of business.

4. Under what conditions is it acceptable for an employee to take merchandise, supplies, and the like?

5. How might you, as a beginning worker, learn the unwritten code of behavior that prevails in your workplace?

6. You may have heard of "padding" an expense account. To pad means to "increase with unnecessary or fraudulent matter." What are some schemes that dishonest employees might use to pad their expense accounts? What do employers do to guard against expense account padding?

7. What is the difference between a gift and a bribe? Give examples to illustrate the distinctions you make.

8. Review the examples of petty bribery presented in this chapter. For each, write a short essay in which you take a stand and defend it, with respect to the ethics of the situation.

9. The text mentions the fact that young people, especially when not closely supervised, are likely to waste time. What are some possible reasons for this? As a supervisor, what might you do to overcome this problem?

10. Interview several employers to determine their expectations regarding loyalty of employees. Then, summarize the employers' expectations and review them with several employees (not necessarily in the same company). Do you find any differences? Are there any possible conflicts that might result from the differences between employee and employer views of loyalty?

11. You come upon two of your co-workers hugging and kissing in the stockroom during working hours. What should you, as a friend and co-worker, do about it? If you were the supervisor, what would you do?

Case Problems

1. Out the Back Door and in the Front.

Assume you have discovered that some of the employees in the supermarket where you work are stealing empty soft drink containers and selling them to youngsters in the neighborhood at half their value. You see some of these children selling the same bottles at the checkstand of your store.

1. What are your responsibilities to your employer? To your co-workers?
2. What should the store manager do upon discovering the details of this situation?

2. To Draw or Not to Draw.

Tim is working part-time in the drafting department of a small manufacturing firm. Since he has access to graphic supplies, materials and equipment, he decides to use his coffee breaks and lunch periods to design and produce detailed sketches of a family room remodeling project for his home.

1. Should Tim ask permission or should he feel free to go ahead with the project, since he intends to do it on his own time?
2. How do you think his supervisor should respond if Tim asks permission?
3. What reasons might be given to justify refusing Tim's request?

3. Business Within a Business.

Bertha works as an assembler in a sash and door factory. Scrap wood accumulates as the window and door frames are produced, and the owner of the business allows the employees to take the discarded wood for use in their fireplaces at home. Bertha's neighbor, Mr. Larson, offers to pay Bertha for fireplace wood, and makes it clear that he will not mention the fact that he is paying Bertha for the wood. Bertha reasons that this is okay. She thinks, "The boss doesn't need to know. Anyway, I'm underpaid on this job, and I can use the extra cash."

1. Do you agree with Bertha's reasoning? Explain your answer.
2. Under what circumstances, if any, would you expect Bertha's employer to approve of this arrangement?

4. How Much is Too Much?

Shirley supervises the shipping and receiving department of a university library. She has several part-time student helpers. Usually, they are able to keep up with the flow of incoming mail. However, after weekends or holidays the books and magazines pile up and it may take several days for Shirley and her crew to get caught up. Most Mondays and days after holidays Shirley works from one to three hours overtime to catch up.

1. Since Shirley works on a salary, she gets no overtime pay. Should she continue working overtime? If not, how should she handle the situation?
2. Shirley catches the flu and misses three days of work. When she returns she finds the backlog of undelivered mail so great that she has to work eleven hours per day for a week. Her supervisor does not seem to know about Shirley's overtime work. What should she do? At what point do you think Shirley should refuse to work overtime?

5. The Encounter.

Hal worked the late night shift as an admitting clerk in a hospital. About 3:00 a.m. he heard a noise in the pharmacy. He opened the door and saw Mr. Swann, the hospital administrator, with a beaker of clear liquid in his hand. Mr. Swann said nothing when he saw Hal. He simply set the beaker on the counter, walked past Hal and out the door. Hal checked the beaker and found it to contain alcohol. Thinking it was none of his business, and fearing that he might be fired if he said anything, Hal said nothing to anyone about the incident. Two months later Mr. Swann was replaced as administrator, with no explanation. But everyone on the hospital staff figured out the reason when Hal admitted him to the hospital later as an emergency case— for alcohol poisoning.

1. Did Hal make the right choice in keeping quiet about the incident? If not, what should Hal have done?
2. If Mr. Swann had caught Hal in the pharmacy with a beaker of alcohol, would he have overlooked the incident? If not, should he have overlooked it?

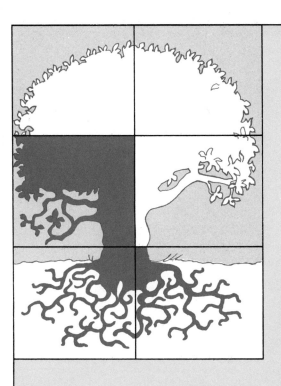

PART THREE

Attitudes

Chapter 5
Developing a positive attitude

There is one person you can make fun of without having some organized group send you nasty letters. There is one person you can "get tough with" without fear of reprisal. There is, in fact, one person whom you can change. That person is yourself.

The mere changing of your own attitudes is a remarkably enlightening experience. If you have been having trouble with your supervisor, if you feel you have been criticized too much and too often, you—being human—have probably tried to get even. Perhaps you have been sullen; you may have answered abruptly; or you may have threatened to quit. What would happen if, instead, you said sincerely, "I know I made an error. You are absolutely right to tell me about it. Is there anything I can do to correct this mistake?" No matter how terrible your supervisor may be, the response to this remark would hardly fail to be less than reasonably positive. Chances are the response will be, "That's all right. YOU CAN CHANGE YOURSELF. We'll forget it this time."

You Can Change Yourself

Changing yourself is the best kind of reforming you can possibly do. But how should you start? What faults do we all have in common? Everyone is an individual. How can we draw

Illus. 5–1.   Behavior Modification: Promote Positive Attitudes in Others

up rules for self-improvement that will be applicable to everyone? Well, there is one trait that most of us can improve. We can all learn to have a positive attitude. Or do you think you already have a positive attitude? Perhaps you do; but you will be unique, indeed, if you do not occasionally say something uncomplimentary about a co-worker or grumble and complain about (1) the weather; (2) your work; (3) your teacher or supervisor; (4) your grades or your pay, among other things.

At a lecture on human relations, the speaker was giving the audience some rules for living. One of the rules was to stop expecting perfection in this world. A member of the audience immediately raised a hand and snapped, "What's wrong with being a perfectionist?" The speaker smiled and answered, "Your tone of voice when you asked that question, for one thing."

Everyone is negative some of the time. Negative feelings, negative attitudes, negative words—all are depressors of the spirit. They all take us—and our hearers—down instead of up. The main thing that is wrong with a negative attitude or statement is that negatives are contagious. You know, yourself, that you can get up in the morning feeling great. Yet, if you meet four or five friends during the day who tell you of depressing happenings, who complain about their lot, or—worst of all— who criticize you and call attention to your mistakes, your happy mood will soon disappear. The other side of the coin is just as contagious, however. Although you may be tired and discouraged, your mood changes when you meet someone who gives you a sincere compliment or who greets you with a smile.

We should be climbing toward happiness or, at least, we would like to think we could do so. Think of happiness as lying at the top of a long stairway with unhappiness at the bottom. Each negative thought or word would take us one step down. Each positive thought or word would take us one step up.

How can you tell if you need to work on this negative habit? Let's try an experiment. Pick a three-hour period when you are usually free to say what you think. From six to nine in the evening is often a time of relative freedom, or from three to six on a Sunday afternoon. Arm yourself with a scratch pad and a pencil. Every time you think or say something negative, write it down. This means *everything,* including, "Is it hot enough for you?" or "You shouldn't wear so much jewelry." Just plain, ordinary negative things that all of us say and think. At the end of the three-hour period, read them over. You will be surprised, first of all, at the number of items you have written. Then you will wonder when you had time to say or do *anything* positive, which may explain why some of us don't do more things of a positive nature.

Accent The Positive

A negative attitude usually creeps up on us because it is so easy to be negative. It takes no effort to let a feeling of self-pity steal over you. There are disappointments in every day. The easy way is to let them engulf us. It does take effort to replace negative thoughts with positive ones, but it is time and effort well spent. The way to start is to take the first steps towards being positive:

Smile. If you make yourself turn the corners of your mouth up instead of down, it will be easier to think of something positive to say. Make a real effort to look pleasant and interested in what is going on around you. You know, under the stimulation of your own interest, those around you may become interesting!

Say Something Pleasant. There are many people in the world who never say anything pleasant. So, for your second step, think of something positive, good-natured, or complimentary to say to someone else at every opportunity. This will do wonders for those around you, but it will also keep you so busy thinking of positive things to say that you won't have time to be negative.

Change Your Negative Statements to Positive Ones. The third step is to change your negative statements in midstream. Say a co-worker reaches into the closet and knocks your best coat on the floor. Without thinking, you start to say, "Why can't you watch what you're doing?" But you catch yourself before you get that far. Instead you say, "Why can't—I help you find what you want?" At first you may think of this as being insincere. But keep it up for at least a week. Start a "Let's be more positive" campaign. Watch yourself. When you start to complain about a teacher, an assignment, the weather, or your financial state, stop. See if you can twist that statement around so that it will be positive. You may be surprised at the way your relationships with people improve.

Change a Negative Problem Into a Positive Situation. After you have practiced on positive statements for a week, you are ready to attack a negative problem. Look around you for some negative situation. Is there a co-worker you dislike? Is there a friend who rubs you the wrong way? Whatever it is, try the positive approach. Try to change the situation by being positive.

Let's say you have a friend, Jeff, who gets on your nerves. He talks about himself all the time. He boasts about everything— his car, his job, his school. You think that, without a doubt, he is the most conceited person you ever met. You may think, "What can I say that is positive that he hasn't already said over and over?" That doesn't matter. Say it anyway. You meet him at lunch and you don't even have time for a greeting before he starts right in to tell you about a test on which he knew all the answers. Why not say, "Jeff, I wish I had your confidence." If you keep out the sarcasm and say it sincerely, this may cause Jeff to stop and think a minute. He may not have too much confidence, and his bragging helps boost his self-confidence. He may say, "To tell you the truth, I have always thought you were the confident one." If something like this should happen, the hostility on both sides will begin to evaporate. Now you're probably thinking, "But how do I know this is the way it would go?" No one knows exactly how a conversation will go. It has been proven, however, that this kind of approach results in a positive reply nearly all the time.

Your campaign to become more positive will get you over a big hurdle. When you learn to look at problems with a positive attitude, you can begin to solve them more easily.

Use Behavior Modification

A more positive attitude will surely make a difference in your campaign to change yourself. It will do even more. In Chapter Two you were introduced to *behavior modification* as a way of developing your self-esteem. You can use a combination of positive attitudes and behavior modification to change others. Most psychologists are convinced that personality is *caused.* You were not born with a chip on your shoulder. That chip came about because of the way someone else treated you.

In a pyschology class this theory was tested in the following experiment. One of the students in the class was unpopular. The student was a loner and did not mix with the other students. Two students in the same class wanted to see if they could cause a personality change. They decided to show the first student lots of attention for a few weeks. They talked to their classmate at every opportunity, treating the classmate as they would a popular person. After a few weeks of this attention, a new personality began to appear. The unpopular student actually became popular; talking more freely, laughing with the others, and feeling at ease with the other students. In short, the student became the kind of person the two experimenters had been pretending the student was. Soon, in fact, the original experimenters had a hard time finding their classmate with any free time for them.

The reason for the change in the student's personality was *reinforcement,* a word meaning reward. The student was rewarded for being popular even before becoming popular. The reward worked just as well as it would have if the student had been given a prize for being the most popular person in the class. This theory, called behavior modification, means that if we want someone to change, we must make changing worthwhile. If you feel unhappy and someone asks you why you look so sad, you may feel comforted but you are not likely to change. But if someone says, "You look so nice in that blue outfit. It accents your blue eyes," you may find yourself feeling happier.

The rule of reinforcement says that people act in ways that bring some kind of reward. If you want to change your behavior, you must have some payoff, some reward. You will not change if no one notices what you have done. Being ignored is painful. If what you do results in indifference, you stop doing it. You know, yourself, that you need to have someone pay attention to you. If you can't get attention for being good, you'll try getting attention by being bad. You can stand anything but indifference.

This is one of the reasons why punishing has never helped much in changing behavior. Punishment is a kind of attention. If you want attention and the only kind you can get is punishment, you will behave in such a way that you will be punished. Punishment is better than no attention at all.

Someone has said that there are three kinds of people in this world: those who make things happen, those who watch others making things happen, and those who don't realize anything is happening. You will have a happier and more effective life if you can turn yourself into the kind of person who makes things happen.

A Positive Attitude at Work

Ms. Nelson and Mr. Yamamoto were chatting at the weekly Rotary Club luncheon meeting. "We had to let three of our young people go last week," said Ms. Nelson, "not because they could not do the work, but because of their attitudes." "I know exactly what you mean," responded Mr. Yamamoto. "We have the same problem in our firm." Mrs. Pitts, overhearing the conversation, interjected, "What *do* you mean? I'm interested to know what you have in mind when you talk about good and bad attitudes in workers."

One of the important factors in success is your attitude toward your job. Every beginner has a lot to learn, but if your attitude is favorable, you will learn faster and your learning time will be accepted by others. If you complain, if you say it can't be done, you will be defeating yourself. A positive work attitude can be the difference between success and mediocrity.

No one likes to be around a negative person. If you like your work, you will have a positive attitude; if you dislike it, your attitude will be negative. If that is what makes the difference at work, then, how can you display a positive work attitude?

Enthusiasm

A good work attitude includes enthusiasm, both for the work and for the firm that employs you. Enthusiasm is actually nothing more than positive energy. When you are enthusiastic, you may seem to accomplish miracles. And the best part of enthusiasm is that it is catching. If you are enthusiastic, a co-worker may find that "down-in-the-dumps" feeling has disappeared. Enthusiasm is a trait that contributes a major share to what goes into success.

Illus. 5–2. Contribute to your success through a positive attitude.

Datatrol, Inc.

Willingness to Learn

A beginner does have a lot to learn. People expect it. They do not expect the learning process to go on forever, though. The beginner who needs to be told something only once is considered unusually bright, and the one who learns new routines and facts without being told is rare, indeed. Everyone makes mistakes, but the beginner with a good work attitude seldom makes the same mistake twice.

Getting Along With People

Perhaps the most important factor in a positive work attitude is getting along with people. This involves understanding yourself, the other person, and the way you choose to influence the other person. Where do you begin? Begin with the most difficult part—understanding yourself.

You may wonder why understanding yourself is more difficult than learning how to influence others. The answer lies in
the years that you have been fooling yourself. You look at yourself through rose-colored glasses. All of us can see the faults
of others, but we cannot see our own. Or, if we do see them,
we "rationalize"—find excuses for the unattractive sides of our
personalities and our characters. So the first step is to take a
good look at yourself.

The next step is to look for something to like in that person
with whom you wish to get along. Liking *something* in others
must precede having the other person like you. It may seem
an oversimplification, but much of getting along with people
consists of just such turnabouts. If you want to be liked, you
must like others. To be *interesting,* you must be *interested*—in the
other person's ideas, problems, and suggestions. If you want
others to adjust to your wishes, you must first learn to adjust
to theirs. Others will overlook your failings more readily if you
develop tolerance toward their failings.

Cheerfulness

No single trait will so endear you to your co-workers and
your supervisors as the ability to look on the bright side, to
deal with others with a light touch. Cheerfulness is a virtue,
even though we seldom hear anyone preach about it, and it is
one that makes working well with others remarkably simple.
Don't take things too hard, keep a light touch, and your work
with others will be smooth and successful.

Actually, cheerfulness is the result of being able to accept
yourself and to accept others. When you can take off your mask,
when you can be your own self, you will have no need for
the defenses you have built up to hide your real self from the
world. When you accept yourself, you also discover that most
of your troubles happen because of what you do. You take things
hard when you are concerned too much with yourself.

When you can change, when you can become more cheerful,
you will be able to think of other people more, and less of
your own shortcomings. Cultivate the light touch; learn to be
cheerful. It only takes practice.

No More Self-Pity

Besides being more positive in what we say, we must get rid of another bad habit—self-pity. Let's wipe out once and for all the "poor little me" feeling. You may have heard the old proverb about the person who complained about having no shoes until that person met someone else with no feet. This is the way to erase those self-pitying thoughts that will—unless we are on guard—creep into our minds. There is too much self-pity in the world, and it is followed by an even more destructive emotion—resentment.

One way to cure resentment is through action. Don't just sit there and brood. Do something! Any kind of positive action will help eliminate resentment, but the best cure is action that you enjoy. Perhaps you have done poorly on a test and you deeply resent the person who got the top grade. Thinking about your resentment—nursing it to keep it warm—will not help; neither will additional study while you are in a resentful mood. Instead, do something you enjoy that is active. Play tennis, join a square dance group, swim, go for a ride on your motorcycle—anything that is fun for you. Combining action with enjoyment will overcome any resentment and put the original cause for resentment in proper perspective.

Overcome Objectionable Habits

Just as there are habits and techniques you should cultivate for success in the world of work, so there are habits that you should avoid. Unfortunately, most of these unwelcome habits never slip into our awareness. You may notice them in others but fail to recognize that you may be guilty, too.

Most of the following objectionable habits come under the heading of bad manners. You may not realize that you have some bad habits, but certainly you should make an effort to correct any faults once they have been called to your attention. Ask a close friend to check you against the following list—and you do the same for your friend. Then make a sincere effort to eliminate any that you do—even occasionally.

Drumming or tapping with fingers, toes, or a pencil
Humming or whistling under your breath

Illus. 5–3. Discover and overcome your objectionable habits.

Sniffling or snorting
Breathing noisily
Blowing your nose noisily
Clearing your throat with a rasp
Sucking your teeth
Coughing or sneezing without turning your face and covering your mouth
    with a handkerchief
Coughing loudly
Fussing with your hair
Playing with rings, beads, or other jewelry
Adusting your collar, cuffs, belt, or the like unnecessarily
Scratching your hair or picking at your face
Chewing gum
Yawning
Backslapping
Whispering when others are speaking
Wrinkling your brows
Slamming doors
Banging telephone receivers
Dashing in and out of rooms

When you know which of the objectionable habits are to
be eliminated from your habit structure, start on just one at

first. When it is eliminated, go on to the second. To eliminate an undesirable habit: (1) be conscious that you possess it, (2) honestly desire to get rid of it, and (3) stop it *now.*

Before beginning this improvement campaign, resolve to be objective about the whole thing, and do not feel hurt when your friend checks an item that is surprising to you. Remember, we are seldom aware of our own bad habits.

Chapter Two described the process by which you can improve your self-esteem and increase your chances for success. Self-esteem works on *you* from within. A positive attitude, as explained in this chapter, works on *others.* As your positive attitude develops, the people around you begin to respond accordingly. They think of you as being enthusiastic, willing to learn, cheerful, and easy to get along with. Their improved image of you causes them to expect positive, productive behavior. As you sense these positive expectations, your motivation to live up to your image is increased. Your self-assurance is increased. The principles of behavior modification begin to work on you and the result is a cycle of reinforcement and improvement, even greater appreciation of your positive attitude, and even higher levels of self-esteem. And, in addition to the beneficial effect of your positive attitude on your own behavior, you find yourself in a new position of power. The influence of your positive attitude on other people allows you to influence *them.* This is particularly true when you apply the principles of behavior modification to change other people in positive ways—to help them improve their self-esteem and positive attitudes.

Questions and Projects

1. Is there somebody that really bothers you—your roommate, a friend, a relative, a co-worker? For a change, be positive and don't nag them or complain about it. Instead, see if you can change their behavior. Use the positive reinforcement approach and compliment them for appropriate behavior. While doing this, you must ignore the behavior that annoys you. Use the following plan:

   a. Describe in detail the situation you wish to improve.
   b. Formulate in detail your plan to increase praise and decrease criticism. Write out some positive statements you might use for example. Using "P" as a symbol each time you praise and "C" each time

you criticize, record your campaign on a calendar for a full week.
  c. At the end of the week, report the results. Can you see a change
      in behavior?

2. Keep a list of all the positive statements you make during one
hour. Time the project so that it is on the same day of the week
and the same time of day. If your new number of positive statements
is the same (or fewer) than before, try the experiment again the next
day. Do this until you form the habit of the positive approach.

3. Behavior modification, as described in this chapter, requires that
you provide yourself with rewards for your positive behavior. This project can help you identify some possible ways of rewarding yourself.
First, choose some way in which you want to change, to improve.
You may decide to study more industriously or to do a better job in
your work. You may decide to work on an emotional or physical fitness
problem. You may decide to diet. Whatever improvement you choose,
fill in a contract like the one shown. But before you do that, it may
be helpful for you to concentrate on identifying some rewards that
will provide the strong motivation you will need to live up to your contract with yourself. First of all, make a "checksheet" on a separate
piece of paper such as the one shown below. Then study the items
listed. Choose those that bring you joy or pleasure, rate them with
respect to the extent of enjoyment, and make a list of the items you
checked "Much" or "Very Much." Then you will be ready to complete
the "Behavior Contract" which follows.

		Extent of Enjoyment		
		Some	*Much*	*Very Much*
1.	Listening to Music			
	a. Popular			
	b. Folk			
	c. Rock			
	d. Rhythm and Blues			
	e. Show Tunes			
	f. Disco			
	g. Jazz			
	h. Country Western			
	i. Classical			
	j. Religious			
2.	Solving Problems			
	a. Working on a Car			
	b. Doing Crossword Puzzles			
	c. Building Models			
	d. Solving Computer Math Problems			

3. Food
   a. Candy   _____
   b. Ice Cream   _____
   c. Cookies   _____
   d. Fruit   _____
   e. Nuts   _____
4. Beverages
   a. Coffee   _____
   b. Tea   _____
   c. Soft Drinks   _____
   d. Milk   _____
5. Participating in Sports
   a. Football   _____
   b. Basketball   _____
   c. Baseball   _____
   d. Tennis   _____
   e. Golf   _____
   f. Swimming   _____
   g. Track   _____
   h. Bowling   _____
   i. Other Sports   _____
6. Watching Sports   _____
7. Reading
   a. Newspapers   _____
   b. Magazines   _____
   c. Adventure   _____
   d. Mystery   _____
   e. Love Stories   _____
   f. Sports   _____
   g. Humor   _____
   h. History   _____
   i. Travel   _____
8. Outdoor Life
   a. Camping   _____
   b. Hiking   _____
   c. Bicycling   _____
   d. Motorcycling   _____
   e. Skiing   _____
   f. Boating   _____
   g. Fishing   _____
   h. Hunting   _____
   i. Walking   _____
   j. Snowmobiling   _____
   k. Horseback riding   _____
9. Entertainment
   a. Radio   _____
   b. Movies   _____
   c. TV   _____

  d. Concerts   _____
  e. Theater   _____
10. Dancing
  a. Discotheque   _____
  b. Ballet or Modern   _____
  c. Ballroom   _____
  d. Folk   _____
  e. Square   _____
11. Playing a Musical Instrument _____
12. Painting or Modeling   _____
13. Sewing   _____
14. Shopping   _____

Now you are prepared with a list of possible rewards. To complete your contract you will need to type or write a form like the one shown below. Include your name on the first line.

  Fill in the number of days in which the contract is to be in effect. On the line beginning BEHAVIOR write the *one* change you are going to work on. On the line beginning REWARDS, list one or more of the activities you selected as being the most enjoyable to you. On the line beginning PENALTIES, list one or more of the enjoyable activities you will give up if you do not live up to your contract.

BEHAVIOR CONTRACT

  I, _____ , do hereby enter into the following agreement with myself. I will perform the behavior stated below for a period of _____ days. In return, I will receive the rewards listed below.

    BEHAVIOR _____
    REWARDS _____

    If I fail to live up to this contract, these penalties will take effect.
    PENALTIES _____

      _____
             Signature

4. Another way of giving yourself rewards is by the token system. With this system you give yourself a check mark for each day that you live up to your contract. Then you give yourself the reward when you have earned a certain number of check marks. No penalty is needed when you use the token reward system. However, you will need a calendar or a progress chart on which to record the check marks you earn. With the token reward system you will fill in the contract in the same way, except that you decide the number of check marks you must accumulate in order to earn the reward.

5. Take a destructive emotion (other than worry) that gives you problems. Describe it, show what it does to people, give an example, and then list as many ways of controlling it as you can.

6. Suppose you were in a conversation with several co-workers at a coffee break. Mr. Sutro has just said he can't stand Miss Wilson, the supervisor. Realizing this is not the kind of talk that should continue, you decide to change the conversation. What would you say? How would you include the previous speaker so he would not be offended?

7. Practice being cheerful until cheerfulness becomes a fixed part of your personality. Act and look cheerful, no matter how you feel. Stand up straight; smile at everybody; look like the world is yours. Try this exercise for one week and report the results.

8. Each Monday afternoon, make a list of the negative statements you make during a three-hour period. Try to keep the time of day the same each week. Also, after you have become more proficient, make a list of the negative statements you change to positive ones, and finally a list of the positive statements you make. See if you can eliminate the negative habit in six weeks.

9. Deliberately choose the most difficult person you know, and begin a campaign to improve the relationship between the two of you. Once a week, write the extent of progress you have made. Date each report.

10. Quick judgments are sometimes made without knowing all of the facts of the case. Make a list of negative statements made to you by others. Opposite the statements, write what you believe may have caused the person to be negative. If possible, learn the *real* reason for each negative statement and compare it against what you *thought* was the reason.

11. For one day, casually express appreciation for everything that is done for you. If anyone opens a door, helps you carry anything, passes you the sugar, or is of assistance in any other way, say, "Thank you," and smile. Report to the class whether it made your day any more pleasant.

12. This week, every time a person says anything to you of a complimentary nature say, "Thank you." Force yourself to do this.

13. This week, casually compliment five of your co-workers or classmates. Keep your words and tone casual—but not sarcastic.

14. Write down five negative statements you have made recently. Can you think of more positive language you might have used? Do you think a more positive approach would have improved the situation? Discuss.

15. Write a short "thank you" note for some favor that has been done you in the past year. Keep the note short, sincere, and conversational. (If you are unable to think of any favors done you, write a "thank you" note to a member of your family.) *And mail the note.*

16. For one week, keep a record of your moods. Each night before you retire, write down which of the following phrases best described your prevailing mood that day:

Very happy	Somewhat depressed
Moderately happy	Very depressed
Neither happy nor depressed	

At the end of the week, see if you need to work on your emotional habit patterns.

Case Problems

1. Shyness.

Mr. Holmes, a bookkeeper from a small town, has found no friends in the office in the city where he is employed. He has been away from home for three years, but he is still homesick. He is very lonely and does not know whether to stay in the city or go back to his hometown. It seems to him that everyone in the office shuns him; they have never asked him to join in any group activities.

1. Is it possible that Mr. Holmes is to blame for the attitude of others toward him?
2. Assume that Mr. Holmes has talked to you about his problem. What would you advise him to do in order to break out of his shell? Be specific.

2. Criticism Trap.

Sarah Dornbush is a student in the local community college. Only a few of Sarah's former high school friends are attending the college. One of these is Sarah's best friend, Chris, who is popular with the other students but who seems to take delight in putting Sarah down. Whenever Sarah meets a new friend, Chris makes some critical remark about the friend to Sarah. Even though Sarah realizes that she should not let Chris' criticism affect her, Sarah usually breaks off with the new friend. Sarah also notices that she is becoming critical of the other students, especially of their clothes, hair length, and general actions. Sarah seems to be "catching" Chris' negative attitude toward strangers. Suggest a solution to the case from Sarah's point of view.

Chapter 6
Motivation

What is self-motivation? Is it busy work? Or is it rather a drive within yourself to get things done? How can you acquire this drive if you do not possess it now? As needs change, the spark that motivates you will change also. Right now, you may be working for grades—a passing grade or a high one. Or you may be interested in the approval of someone whose opinion is important to you. These motivating influences are what we call "external" or "extrinsic" ones. This means that the spur to achieve comes from the outside. In time, this external motivation may be partly replaced by "internal" motivation, the kind that comes from within, such as the satisfaction that comes from doing a good job.

When you are internally motivated in most things, you will find accomplishment much easier. Most of us, however, never quite reach the point where we care nothing for the praise or commendation of others. This stage of need fulfillment is sometimes called *self-realization*. Consider it an ideal that, some day, you may attain. In the meantime, try to find some motivating influence that will work for you, that will help to keep you from wasting time, from making excuses to yourself—in short, from lacking in industry.

Illus. 6–1. Motivation: Going the Extra Mile

Taking Initiative and Being Resourceful

Vivian and Paul are taking a shorthand course. Vivian studies each day, completing all the homework that is required for the class, plus practices with the set of tapes the instructor has placed on "reserve" in the library. She competes with herself to try to improve her speed and accuracy. Paul, on the other hand, merely does the work that is required. He feels that if the instructor felt the tapes were worthwhile, they would be part of the required work. Which student is demonstrating good self-motivation?

Initiative means the energy, or aptitude displayed in the action that tends to develop new fields: self-reliance; originality; enterprise; resourcefulness. You can hardly read such a definition without thinking of the selling field. The successful salesperson *must* have initiative. As a salesperson you must think of new methods of reaching your customers; you must sometimes seek out new customers; you must stress the new features of your merchandise. Initiative is a central trait in selling, but it is useful in all business jobs. When you are a beginner in many occupations, you may not find many important situations calling for the use of initiative. The first job calls for following orders implicitly, doing what you are told to do without question. In time, though, you will grow through experience and practice. You will then be given larger responsibilities and demands that call for independent thinking and action.

Use Good Judgment

When to use initiative, as well as how much to use, calls for the use of your own good judgment. Again, put yourself in your employer's place. How would you like your employee to proceed? The new salesperson should not rearrange displays so they will look more attractive. This may be viewed by some supervisors as showing too much initiative. On the other hand, failure to act in a crisis when there appears to be no precedent may be even worse. For instance, if a customer is upset upon receiving merchandise other than that ordered, as a salesperson you should certainly show your concern. You should say that something will be done about the situation whether you had been previously instructed to do so or not.

Illus. 6–2. Take the initiative and be resourceful.

Rick Reinhard

   As a newcomer in the business world, you may find it troublesome to know just how far you should go in the matter of
doing things on your own. Sometimes the rules of the organization make it necessary to follow a set pattern in everything that
is done. In most cases, however, the follow-the-rules phase lasts
only a short time. Before long you will be faced with an emergency. The executive who is to sign all orders is in the hospital
or out of town. When something of this nature happens, the
only thing you can do is weigh the matter carefully. What would
be the results if you followed the rules? Would you lose an
order? Would you cause a visiting executive to take the wrong
plane? If the consequences of following the rules are worse, in
your judgment, than acting on your own, you must have enough
initiative to act on your own. The only requirement is that you
think the situation through carefully, making your decision on
the basis of facts and objectives and not on panic.
   Resourcefulness is a help at any level of business. If you
can make do with whatever is at hand, you are being resourceful.

You are resourceful if you can look ahead to possible conse-quences of two actions and choose the one more likely to meet with success. If fact, the motto THINK will help you be more resourceful.

Be willing to work. It may seem redundant to explain that a worker must be willing to work. But many workers seem to spend their time in other ways. There are, however, a number of clues to tell your supervisor or employer how willing a worker you are. You willingly perform the task that is assigned to you. After the assignment has been made, you arrange your duties so that the work is completed on time. Because mistakes can be serious, you take great pains to be accurate. You take pride in your work and the finished product has a careful, painstaking look.

Learn On Your Own

You will be showing initiative by learning all you can about the business and your place in it. Initiative is also shown when you find additional tasks to do when your assigned work is finished, by taking courses to prepare yourself for promotion, and by going ahead with work that must be done even though it has not been definitely assigned to you. Initiative is displayed also by learning how to think and act swiftly in emergencies and by doing more than you are told to do. If new and unusual situations arise, aside from your regular routine, you should han-dle them.

You will show initiative if you are able to take another employee's place without detailed instruction. You should be able to apply information received in one situation to a similar situation. You will plan and carry out new duties with a mini-mum of help from others. You will attempt constructive creative work.

Learn to handle all telephone calls adeptly and to arrange conferences to the satisfaction of both or all persons concerned. Experience will enable you to determine whether your employer should be called at home if an important customer appears unex-pectedly.

If you are alert, original, and determined to see opportunity and to make the most of it, you will learn to take advantage of situations by a display of initiative. The person who is enthusiastic about putting new ideas into effect does not say, "It can't be done." Nor does the person bother superior officers with trifling matters or wait to be told what to do. Nor will the person need to have work laid out or to be told repeatedly how to perform a task. Do not let new and unfamiliar situations upset you. Through the use of initiative, let them be stepping-stones to greater efficiency.

The Extra Mile

What does "going the extra mile" mean to you? Many years ago, the word "character" was in common use. Character meant the ability to remain steadfast under difficulties; and, in that bygone day, strength of character was the most important attribute that an individual could possess. Now, however, we don't hear much about character; the word seems actually to have gone out of fashion. In its place, let's substitute "going the extra mile."

How do you know if you can go the extra mile? One clue is this: Can you keep going when the going gets rough? Another clue is whether you can stand on your own two feet. People who lean on others, who always ask for help, who are filled with self-pity are not the kind who go the extra mile. They are the ones who give up. All people have problems; but those who can go the extra mile master their problems.

It takes courage to go the extra mile. It also takes courage to admit your mistakes. Once having admitted them, however, you will find your path much smoother. If, on the other hand, you cover up your mistakes, you will spend far too much time making excuses, blaming your troubles on others, depending on the alibi. If you admit an error in judgment, you may feel ashamed—or you may even be punished—but eventually you will be respected for your honest admission.

You demonstrate your ability to go the extra mile by taking responsibility for your errors, by facing irritations without reacting to them, by defending the policies of the firm, by ignoring pettiness and gossip that may involve you, by standing up to be counted for that which you know is right. You go the extra mile when you cheerfully perform the difficult, tedious, or unpleasant task when it falls to you. You go the extra mile when you perform your work with poise, dignity, and patience al-though conditions at work or in your private life may be distress-ing. You go the extra mile when you do not take unnecessary advantage of illness, physical handicaps, or interruptions to avoid work.

The strong person is rarely rewarded early in a career. You should prepare yourself for the fact that, like the reward for many other positive qualities, the reward for going the extra mile may be delayed. Still, if you are really the person who goes the extra mile, your own self-knowledge will be reward enough. You will know that you can cope with whatever you need to do. Eventually, others will know that in a crisis, great or small, they can depend on you.

Put Your Adult Self In Control

In Chapter 1, the three selves each of us has inside us were discussed. The Adult self is the self that is strengthened when you go the extra mile. The Adult self is then able to take control. When you have a strong Adult self, you will refuse to become ruffled, no matter what the provocation. Anyone in business who can remain calm under pressure becomes a valuable asset to the firm. You see, emotions are contagious; both hysteria and tranquility are catching. Modern business is filled with emergen-cies, crises, pressures. Someone who can remain calm will act as a human tranquilizer to others. If you are able keep your control when those about you are losing theirs, you will be a real addition to the staff of the firm.

An Adult self in control has another side, as well. Not only will it help you deal with negative emotions, but it will act as a self-starter to make yourself do the things you should do. Actually, your success in business will depend to a great extent upon your ability to develop good work habits. Inborn intelli-gence is highly overrated by many people as a factor in success. A brilliant mind helps, of course, but it will not ensure success. Interest in your work, enthusiasm, work habits, carefulness in checking details—all these play an important part.

You may have observed someone with great talent who was at the top of a profession. What you did not see was the long period of hard work that had gone into this person's career. The axiom that genius is 90 percent perspiration and 10 percent inspiration is true. Even gifted people must work hard if their talent and intelligence are to benefit themselves and others; work always requires self-control. In long-range planning, all of us want to work; but doing the job in front of us requires much personal discipline. If a supervisor oversees the work, this outside force helps you to settle down to work. If you have a job you must do without prodding from others, you must have Adult self-control to work efficiently.

Develop Your Self-Motivation

Some of the common ways to put off applying Adult self-control are used by all of us. We get a drink of water; we adjust the ventilation; we become distracted at the slightest interruption and find it hard to pick up where we left off. All of these preparations for work must be forgotten. The best way to start working is to sit down and begin. Get started with a stubby pencil. Save that drink of water for a reward at the end of your first completed page. Adjust the ventilation as a reward for the completion of your second. If you use Adult self-control the first few times, you will form the habit of concentrated effort. With this habit, you will find yourself becoming a much more productive worker.

There is no simple formula for controlling efforts and emotions. By trial and error you will discover ways that work for you. Just remember that practice in Adult self-control builds strength. The following list will provide you with opportunities for building a strong Adult self. If you find habits in this list that you would like to acquire, begin now to make such habits a part of your own personality.

Ability to work at a task that does not appear to offer immediate interest or pleasure

Ability to work instead of participating in pleasant sports or entertainment when the work cannot be postponed

Not waiting until the last minute before beginning a necessary task

Conquering evidences of anger, impulses to "tell off" other people, and smouldering resentment

Ability to spend some time alone in quiet work or recreation

Ability to work in the presence of distracting influences—physical discomfort, noise, emotional stress, heat, etc.

Ability to work when weary, even late at night if the occasion demands "burning the midnight oil"

Expecting oneself to perform assignments, not just satisfactorily, but well

Ability to take justified correction or criticism without malice, anger, or tears

Ability to tolerate differences of opinion, injustices, and impositions without a display of emotion

Ability to be objective and impartial when working with others, regardless of friendly or unfriendly feelings toward co-workers

Ability not to spend money for something that will give immediate pleasure when the money can be set aside so that it can provide greater satisfaction in the future

Ability not to boast, even though there may be cause

Ability to keep confidential information secret

Want to Grow and to Share

A number of studies have been made of successful young people. One such study asked many questions of young people who had succeeded. In their answers, successful beginning workers said they did not expect success to come to them without effort. They stated that nothing comes to those who only wait for it. They believed that successful people must work hard, adjust to life's problems, want to improve, and make a determined effort to become more capable.

If you have ever tried to reform another person, you have probably discovered what an impossible task it is. The reason for the difficulty lies in a simple fact. Change and growth come to a person because the person wants to change and to grow— not because someone else desires the change. In order to grow, then, you must have a deep desire to grow.

Desire for Improvement

The desire for improvement is a wish to enhance oneself in value or quality. Everyone has vague desires for improvement. With success, however, you become aware of what is involved in achieving greater success and are able to set more realistic goals. For example, the untried student may dream of handling scores of workers with a word. A business person who knows what is involved in leading others, and who knows the difficulties likely to be encountered, will set goals within the realm of possibility. For this very reason, a realistic desire for improvement is usually stronger after the worker has had some success in work.

You probably know someone who is bitter because of lack of success, even though everything the person had been told to do had been done. Unfortunately, however, doing only what you are told to do or meeting the minimum expectations of a job is not enough to bring success.

To be a successful worker you must go beyond the call of duty. You must do what is expected of you—plus. In adding this plus quality that is needed for success, you must not be aggressive or rude. Instead, you should, in a quiet and confident way, give more thought and work to the assignment. This plus quality has two parts. One part is a desire for improvement; the other is doing something about the wish to improve.

The desire for improvement may be expressed in being proud of the growth of your firm, in watching and helping that growth. If you have this pride, you will also be proud of the amount of work you can do in a certain time. One of the joys of any kind of work is pride in good work. Even after the day's work is finished, you can express pride in your work. Read the newspapers and magazines for items that may affect your firm. Keep in touch with current and local affairs.

A desire for improvement is shown in your attitude toward your work. You will welcome and encourage suggestions from your superiors for doing your work more efficiently. You will be alert to suggestions for improving your work when they come from fellow employees. If someone tells you about an unconscious mannerism you have that is making you conspicuous, you make a determined attempt to eliminate it.

Desire to Share

To be unselfish means that you are willing to share, to pay attention to the interests of others, and to be generous with your time and talents. All human traits are found in employers because they are human beings. Yet, while selfishness can be found in the world of work, unselfishness and many other positive qualities can also be found. As an employee, you must be aware of your interests but also aware of the interests of others.

The ability to share is sure to be appreciated by the companies for which you will want to work. All businesses are working hard to create goodwill with their customers and their potential customers. If this same quality is evident among the employees of a firm, it will help them create a good feeling with the public. Sometimes you may see cases where it appears that selfishness is rewarded and unselfishness unnoticed. Such instances do occur, of course, both in the employment community and in all other areas of living. The results of an unselfish attitude toward others will be evident in your personality, however, if you continue this trait. Appreciation of unselfishness may be slow, but it will be sure.

If you have the opportunity, talk with experienced business people about selfishness and unselfishness in business. You will discover that most people have a basic respect for fair play and unselfishness. Your co-workers will dislike you if you violate these basic values. To be accused of unfairness or selfishness would cost you more than any reward you could gain through pursuing these traits.

You may express unselfishness by lending or sharing your materials and equipment with other employees where there is a need. You will give information, time, or services when your department is working under pressure. You will work overtime when this is necessary to complete the job on time. When there are unpleasant duties to be done, you will do your share willingly.

All of these suggestions are familiar to you. Most of us have grown up with such maxims. All that is necessary is to make them habitual actions.

Learn To Share The Glory

There is another side of unselfishness, however, that is not stressed; yet it is even more important to the smooth working of a business team. This side is the ability to accept gracefully the praise that is given your superior when you were largely responsible for the work, the idea, or the plan. Developing this kind of unselfishness is not easy. In our fiercely competitive society most of us try to shine individually; we dislike sharing with others honors rightfully belonging to us. Yet an old saying is true: You can get anything done so long as you don't care who gets the credit.

There are steps in developing this cooperative kind of unselfishness. First, refrain from talking about your high skills, high grades, and successes in general. Rather, help another person to accomplish something and then praise the one you helped. This is the way to begin. After a while you will receive a greater feeling of pleasure from the success of the one you helped than you ever would from your own successes.

From this beginning it is a short step to a glow of pride when others in your department or your company achieve honors in which you had no share. Envy and jealousy—two most unattractive traits—can be eliminated from your nature with this sort of practice. All it takes is practice each day. If you can become the kind of person who is pleased when you hear words of praise for someone else, you will have taken a giant step toward emotional health. Nothing is so destructive to the personality as resentment.

Desire for Civic Sharing

As you grow in your ability to share with your fellow workers, you will need to expand your horizons to the community in which you live and work. You will then have civic or social consciousness, having a desire to further existing institutions if they are working for the public good. If you see a need for change in the local government bodies, you will be willing to do your share to bring such change about. Working for public betterment is one of the hallmarks of an adult person. You know, of course, that business depends on society and that society regulates business. You know, too, that the services of all legitimate institutions have value. You also serve society in your capacity of employee, no matter how humble your position.

When you are called upon to contribute to your United Fund, the Red Cross, and the various other drives, you are glad to do so. The request usually comes through the business that employs you, and that business is judged by the social consciousness of its employees. If you are asked to work for some civic organization for the general good of the community, you are glad to be of help. When requests for information come to you, you answer them promptly and courteously. You obey the laws of your community; you set a good example to others in your conduct and in your speech.

Illus. 6–3. Share your abilities through community service.

Source: Alabama Bancorporation, 1978 Annual Report

As you mature as a worker, you in turn become a leading citizen of the community—one to whom your fellow citizens will turn for leadership. This day will come more quickly if you get the feeling of civic responsibility early—responsibility for those less fortunate than you, responsibility for helping to maintain and carry on the worthwhile institutions of today. Your service to society is a debt you owe in payment for the privileges that are yours.

Questions and Projects

1. What is the difference between "external" motivation and "internal" motivation? Give examples of each. Under which type of motivation is the most work likely to be accomplished? Explain your answer.

2. You work in the produce department of a supermarket. The assistant manager assigns you to make a display of fruit by stacking it to form a pyramid. This takes time and patience. In a trade magazine you read an article in which "informal display" is described, and you come to the conclusion that the formal pyramid display is out of date and inefficient. Should you take the initiative to display the fruit in an informal manner and "surprise" your supervisor?

3. What does it mean to be resourceful? Give examples.

4. You have a problem with spelling the technical words on your new job as a legal secretary. You have been asking a co-worker, Terry, for the spelling of words that give you trouble. Finally, instead of spelling a word for you, Terry (without looking up) points to the dictionary on top of a file cabinet. Is there a message for you in Terry's gesture? What is it?

5. You work in a situation where co-workers are expected to fill in for each other when someone is absent from work. In what ways might you prepare for the time when you will be assigned to fill in for someone else?

6. Is it better to admit your mistakes or to try to cover them up? Under what kinds of circumstances might you want to make it appear that someone else is (at least partly) to blame? In a group discussion, share your experiences to determine what the likely consequences are when you cover up, and when you tell all.

7. Are there any situations in which an "alibi" is better than the candid truth? Discuss this question.

8. Discuss the differences between how your "Adult self" and your "Child self" might behave in emergencies and high pressure situations.

9. List several ways you could improve your self-motivation. From the list, choose the ways in which you could start now.

10. Can you honestly share praise with others? Why do you think you can or cannot?

Case Problems

1. Use of Initiative.

Frank Zwiefel has just completed a report that must be sent out in the afternoon mail. His employer intends to send a letter with the report, but he is called out of the office just before closing time and without having been able to dictate the letter. His employer says nothing to Frank before leaving. Frank knows, however, that the letter will be similar to the one sent the previous month. He decides to type the letter and sign it with his employer's name and his own initials.

1. What would you have done in Frank's position?
2. Which would be more serious, sending the letter without being told or sending the report without a covering letter?
3. If you were Frank's employer, how would you react to having an employee act in this way without instructions?

2. Should You Sleep on It?

Bill Graham, Linda Rozow's employer, is infuriated because of a serious mistake in an order sent in by Tim Yeoman, a sales representative on the road. Bill immediately calls in his secretary and dictates a letter discharging Tim. Because Bill has to leave at once for a meeting, he asks Linda to sign and mail the letter. Linda is aware that her employer is having an off day. Tim is a personal friend of hers, and she knows that up to this time he has been very efficient and well liked, both by his customers and Bill. Instead of transcribing and mailing the letter, she decides to hold it until the next day.

1. What do you think of Linda's action?
2. Should personal friendship enter a business situation of this kind?
3. What chance is Linda taking?
4. Do you think Linda might be motivated by feelings other than friendship for Tim? If so, what are they?
5. In case Bill feels the same way the next day and wants Tim discharged, what should Linda do?
6. Suppose Bill comes in the next morning and tells Linda he has changed his mind and that he is going to call Tim to see if he can talk him into staying with the company?
7. Can you think of a more straightforward way by which Linda could have accomplished the same result?

3. Taking Responsibility.

Alice Limmer, a division manager of a business that distributes its products nationally, has been out of the office for a week. She is in the hospital recovering from an operation and cannot be disturbed with business affairs. The operation was an emergency, and nothing was said about who should make the decisions. Ellen Shafer has just received a large rush order over the telephone from a new local customer whose credit rating has not yet been established. It is the policy of the business that all orders from new customers must have Alice's OK before being delivered.

Ellen takes it upon herself to investigate the credit standing of this new company. She finds it to be excellent. Ellen has three alternatives from which she can choose. She can (1) refuse the order, (2) call and ask if the company can wait for two weeks (when Alice will be well enough to discuss business matters), or (3) approve the order in Alice's name and have the goods delivered.

1. What is Ellen's responsibility in this matter?
2. What is Ellen's authority?
3. Which decision should Ellen make? Why?

Chapter 7
Developing productive work habits

If you have never worked or if you have never put in a full day's work for a day's pay, you will have little conception of what this means. Any job contains a certain amount of routine work, and most of this work is concentrated in the beginning levels. The way to emerge the victor over drudgery is to make your habits work for you. Work habits, like other habits, are built up day by day. It will pay you to form good work habits from the very beginning of your first job.

Dependability

Arnold and Phyllis, two motel managers on their way to lunch, were sharing the "good news" and "bad news" of the day. "I had to let one of my best clerks go today," said Arnold. "But why would you do that," Phyllis asked. "She just wasn't dependable. When she was on the job, she was top-notch. But you can't run a motel when you don't know whether or not your clerks are going to show up." Why do you suppose Arnold was so concerned about dependability that he was willing to fire a competent employee and replace her with one less competent?

Illus. 7–1.   Work Habits: Cultivate Productive Ones

If someone says you are dependable, what does it mean? In most cases, it means you do what you say you will do. It sounds quite simple, doesn't it? Yet workers with the best of intentions are often labeled as undependable. They hate to hurt another's feelings by saying "No." They say they will get the report out by five o'clock, but they really know they won't be able to do it. Dependable people, however, do not say "Yes" unless they are certain they can carry out their promise. In fact, when you say you will do something, you have—in effect— signed a contract. A written contract, of course, would seem more important to you; but a spoken promise is just as important. If you, as a worker, are dependable, you will do your work well. You will not be an alibi artist. If you make a mistake, you will admit it and suggest a way of correcting it; you will suggest a solution. Being dependable also means that you will be at work when you are expected. You will be on time, and you will use your time well.

Attendance and Punctuality

You would very likely consider taking money from the cash register as dishonesty, something you would never do. Yet failure to come to work, tardiness in coming to work, tardiness in returning from lunch periods and coffee breaks are just as serious, just as dishonest as taking money from the cash drawer. Attendance and punctuality are within your power, too. You may be doubtful of your skill, your manners, your appearance; but you need not be doubtful of your ability to get to work every day a few minutes before your work day beings. Attendance and punctuality form an important block in building your success. Don't let this particular block crumble. Be there—and be on time.

Use Your Time Well

When you work, you are paid for your time and the way you spend it. In business, of course, time is money; many of the good work habits you will need involve the proper use of time. For example, you will arrive at work on time—or even a few minutes early—every day. This habit cannot be overstressed. It is important because it shows others that you value your job,

Illus. 7–2. Make your habits work for you.

Campbell Soup Company

but the greatest value in arriving on time is its effect on you. This is best illustrated by what happens when you are late for work. Everything you do becomes shaded by the fact that you were late. You are behind with you work, so you hurry to catch up; because you hurry, you make mistakes; making mistakes causes you to become flustered, so you hurry faster. This circle of hurry and errors goes on all day. On the other hand, if you come to work early, you are relaxed when you start your first task. Relaxation helps you work rapidly and accurately. Working in this way brings you a feeling of satisfaction, and this feeling helps you with the next task at hand. The result is a circle of excellence that works for you all day.

Leaving early should be avoided. Clock watchers seldom get promoted. You are using time that belongs to the company if you leave early for or return late from lunch and coffee breaks, or if you spend extra time talking in the washroom. Time is involved in the rules that govern your work. Whatever the rule may be, you must abide by and not exploit the rule.

Efficiency

Haru Yamamoto and Kevin Melville were seatmates on an airplane trip to a travel agency managers' convention. Haru started the conversation. "How's business, Kevin?" "Best ever, Haru. But I'm a bit worried about how its going to be after next week. My best agent has been hired away by Yamamoto World Travel!" Haru smiled. "I know. And I expect *my* business to improve. We're lucky to get Thelma. In your letter of recommendation, you should not have been so honest." "I wish we could have offered her a management position," Kevin responded. "Thelma is the most *efficient* agent we have. Not the most intelligent. Not the best educated. Not the most experienced. But the most *efficient!*" What do you think are some of the specific skills that made Thelma so special?

One of the most important work habits a worker can possess is efficiency. This means that, first of all, your work place is arranged neatly. Study several examples of neat, efficient layouts. Notice how supplies should be arranged for quick and easy handling. A neatly arranged work station will make *you* more *efficient.* You will be ready to plan and organize materials, supplies, and the work itself so that tasks can be completed as rapidly and as accurately as possible. Efficiency also involves discovering the work standards in your place of employment and working hard to meet them.

One difference between actual employment and school assignments will soon become apparent: Perfection is always desirable, but sometimes must give way to practicality. For instance, if a letter is not centered, you might have to mail it anyway, because time and supplies might be more important than perfection. In other cases, such as machining a part to specific tolerances, you may have to throw away the spoiled part and start over. Being efficient involves judging the relative values of tasks when measured in terms of time, energy, and supplies. These judgments will vary, of course, according to the needs of your particular firm.

Not Losing Excessive Time in Personal Matters

If you are interested in building a reputation for being efficient, you will take care of personal matters on your own time.

When you are at work, you will give your time and your attention to your job. One particular personal matter that should be considered is personal telephone calls. Your company may have strict rules regarding personal telephone calls during working hours but, even if it does not, you should make it a practice to refrain from talking to family and friends during your working day except in cases of emergency. If a friend calls you at work, tell the friend you will call back on your first break or during your lunch hour. If you are a working parent, you may find it necessary to take a personal call if it has to do with your child's welfare. When the need arises, however, try to keep the call short. Use a pay phone rather than tie up the business lines with personal matters.

Visiting with other workers should be discouraged, too. Of course, you will be friendly and pleasant. Greet other workers when you come to work in the morning and when you leave in the evening. But talking over last night's activities or your favorite sport should wait until lunch time or during your break.

Illus. 7–3. Organize your work to become more efficient.

Whatever the rule, do not spend too much time away from your work for any reason. You would not take money from the cash register; neither should you take time from your working day.

Amount of Acceptable Work Produced

Part of your job success is your ability to produce. Speed alone, though, is not the key to efficiency. The way to build up your work production has three parts: (1) an efficient work station, with your tools within easy reach, (2) repeated practice on the parts of the task that slow you down, and (3) an objective that increases as you improve. For example, if you can lay only 40 cement blocks in an hour, try to improve that rate by (1) having the blocks within easy reach and having enough mortar always on hand so that you don't run out. Then (2) repeat laying down just the right amount of mortar if leveling each block is a problem for you, Finally (3) try to lay 45 blocks per hour. Once you have succeeded, see if you can lay 50 blocks in an hour, and so on.

The same procedure can be used with any kind of work. Remember, though, that your objective must be to increase the amount of work while maintaining high quality of work.

Acceptability of Work—Is Within Acceptable Work Standards For This Job

Another test of efficiency is your willingness to keep at a difficult job until you get it right. Willingness to take pains with your work is not spread equally over all different kinds of tasks. For example, you may be happy to retype a page in order to make it neat and free from smudges and noticeable erasures. This same desire for perfection, however, may not work for you when you are asked to go through the files and discard papers that have outlived their usefulness. You may do a sloppy job if you are told to clean up the duplicating room.

Every job has some drudgery in it. You must be willing to take the drudgery with the satisfactions. Be sure you have what it takes to become quality conscious in your work. Pride in your work can be developed; however, it helps if you can find the kind of work where you *want* to take pride in it, where quality is important to you.

Neatness and Orderliness

In Chapter Three, the importance of being neat and orderly with your clothing was discussed. But there is a need for neatness in your work station, as well. Your work must be neat; your desk or counter must be orderly. One way of keeping your work in order is to keep everything you work with in a certain place, where you will be able to find it when you need it. The worker who constantly borrows tools from other workers will soon have trouble finding friends. Neatness may not come easily to you, but it is a habit worth cultivating.

Accuracy

Accuracy is a result of having pride in your work. Employers are always searching for workers who want to do a good job, who have pride in their work. If you are accurate in paperwork, you learn to check everything. You proofread carefully. If you are uncertain of a name or of an address, you look it up in the files or in the telephone directory. If you deal with numbers, you check them carefully. Anyone can make an error; however, you are there to see that no error goes past you.

Thoroughness

Another trait of great value to you on a job is thoroughness. If you are thorough, you finish what you start, you persevere, and you display exactness. It is difficult to impress most beginners with the importance of thoroughness. Good intentions are not enough. Every task entrusted to you in business must be performed completely and accurately. Following through is as necessary in business as it is in tennis or golf.

One habit you should develop is that of thoroughly checking your work. You must be able to evaluate critically the work you do. You must learn to check off details as they are completed. Particularly at the close of the working day, you must check to see that all details have been taken care of before you leave. The rewards in business are reserved for those who do all that is required of them and a little bit more.

If you are selling, you must make out all sales slips completely, accurately, and legibly. If you do bookkeeping work, you must see that each entry in your books is carefully and correctly made. You must be sure that the statements you send out are correct. You must be thorough in making out all reports. You must check the correctness of all data in the correspondence you transcribe and make sure that all questions have been answered. If you have *any* doubts about the meaning or spelling of a word, look it up in the dictionary. Proofread every word of every page you type, and check the enclosures that accompany the correspondence.

Organize Your Work

Another rung on the ladder in your climb to success is the ability to organize a task into manageable units. For example, if Job A and Job B are needed in order to do Job C, you should see that Jobs A and B are done first. Organizational ability becomes more important as you rise higher in your work level. When you take your first job, it will usually be a routine one. Someone else tells you what to do, checks your work, and suggests improvements. As your ability increases, however, you will find that you are trusted more and more to take care of the total job, to decide how you are going to attack the problem. Here is where organizational ability will be needed.

Much of what has been discussed in the preceding chapters will help you become better organized: learning to make decisions quickly, seeing that your work output is high, developing accuracy in your work, and working within the acceptable standards of your job. Now, however, you must learn to do the hard job first. You must eliminate the common habit of putting off until tomorrow what should be done today. Secondly, you must see that all of the papers, drafts, tools, and so on, needed for a single job are kept in one place so that you will not be wasting time looking for the things you need when you start work on that job.

Organizing your work also means planning your work. You must make a plan before you start. If organizing is new to you,

you should write your plan down. First comes the due date. Write down when the job must be completed. Next, divide your task into parts and set a date when each one is to be finished. Third, make sure all of the supplies, papers, answers to questions, and needed calculations are at hand. Then get to work. See that you work on the task the number of hours necessary each day in order to complete the job when it is due.

You may have heard of Parkinson's Laws, one of which states that work expands so as to fill the time available for its completion. You know, yourself, that if you are invited to an exciting party and have just 30 minutes to finish up a task, you'll get it done in 30 minutes. If you have three hours in a lazy afternoon, somehow that same task will take three hours to finish.

Knowing how to organize is the key to beating Parkinson's Law. It consists of nine steps. Let's take them in order. Say you have a big, difficult job to do. Here's how you go about it:

1. Get going right now. Don't wait until you can do a good job. Get started, good job or not, right now.
2. Give yourself a mental reward after your first hour of work. Say, "Hey, that's not bad." You know that praise is the best motivator there is; why not use it to motivate yourself? But keep it strictly to yourself.
3. Try being positive about the job for 10 or 15 minutes at first. Later, you can build your positive mental attitude to 20 minutes, then 30 minutes. Before long you will have developed a positive attitude toward the entire difficult task. Somehow, a positive attitude makes the job go faster and better.
4. Organization doesn't come naturally to most of us. We have to work at it. If you are the creative type, you will have to work harder. Have an exact place for everything with which you work, and put it back in that place as soon as you are finished with it.
5. Don't put off that hard job until a better day comes along. You may think that today is too hectic to start a big, important job; you'll put it off until tomorrow when things will be better. But tomorrow will not be better; it will be worse. You can play a trick on yourself by saying, "I won't do very much on this hard job today; I'll just get started." Somehow, the momentum builds up from getting started, and you may get a big chunk of the job finished the first day.
6. Don't be a "pencil sharpener"—one who wants everything to be perfect before starting to work. The temperature must be just right. The light must be adjusted several times. You are thirsty and decide

to get a drink of water. While you are up, you sharpen six or seven pencils so you won't have to bother sharpening them while you are working. But you needn't have bothered. You never will get to work. There will always be something left to do so that the working environment will be perfect. Instead of being a "pencil sharpener," start with a stubby pencil. Never mind the temperature or the light. Concentrate on your work and you won't notice them. Get a drink of water as a reward for your first 30 minutes of effort. Don't get ready. Get at it!

7. Don't do all the small, easy jobs and get them out of the way and then tackle the big job. You know what happens. By the time you get those small, easy jobs done you're tired—and it's time for your coffee break. Let the easy jobs go. Do the hard job first. Having it off your mind will release all kinds of untapped energy, and you'll be able to polish off those easy jobs in half the time.

8. Don't waste time making decisions over trifles. Learn to make decisions quickly. If the decision is a minor one, flip a coin. Indecision is actually only a bad habit; yet it slows down the "getting things done" potential in all of us beyond belief. By the law of averages, the more decisions you make, the more *right* decisions you have the chance to make. Keep this in mind when indecision threatens to take over.

9. Don't leave your workday to chance. *Plan* each day the night before. If you are the disorganized type, you had better write down your plan. The mere act of writing something down is the first step toward doing it. Also, writing your plan for the next day just before you go to sleep gets your unconscious mind to help. The next day you'll be ready to get at it. Don't think of the difficulties as you plan—how hard the job is, how tired you are, how little you are appreciated. This kind of thinking gets your unconscious mind working against you. Think instead about how you are going to do the task; visualize yourself doing it.

Suggest Improvements in Work Techniques and Operations

Another habit that will contribute to your success is one that must wait until you have established yourself in your job. Even then, it is wise to make suggestions for improving work techniques tactfully. When you can make suggestions without offending other workers or your supervisor, you will have become a real asset to your company. New ideas are always welcome; the danger lies in suggesting your new ideas with a "know-it-all" attitude—and before you have really learned how to do your job efficiently. Remember, though, that business needs new ideas, new techniques, new ways to save time and money. Be willing to offer them without expecting anything in return.

Learn to Work Under Pressure

Finally, we call attention to one of the factors that contribute to your mental health—the ability to work under pressure or abnormal conditions. This means you are able to meet deadlines, keep three or four jobs going at once, do extra work without panic. Of course, you will be better able to work under pressure if your physical health is good, but there is an added factor. Can you remain calm in a crisis? One way to build this added factor is to learn to control your emotions. Sometimes when pressure mounts, it will help to stop for a moment (especially when you feel your muscles tightening up) and take a few deep breaths. Other times you may find it helpful to do a relaxing exercise—swinging your hands at your sides and dropping your head forward. Relaxation, of course, is the key; and many of us must train ourselves in relaxation. If you can find time outside your work to do some of the things you enjoy, you will be better able to work under pressure when the need arises.

Productive work habits are nothing more than ordinary habits applied to work. Once you learn how to make your habits work for you, you will become more productive in your job and more valuable to your employer. Chances are you will even feel better about yourself as well as your work.

Questions and Projects

1. How would you spend your time while waiting for customers: (a) in a dress shop (b) in a bookstore (c) in a drugstore?

2. Time yourself on making decisions. Begin first with little things; what to wear, what to order, what route to take when you go on an errand. Keep a record of how many seconds it takes you to make up your mind. Your eventual goal is to make instant decisions on little things and quick decisions on more important matters.

3. Choose a time-consuming job you must do. Estimate the time it usually takes you to complete the task. Now try to cut the time down

by one half. Continue to time yourself when similar jobs come up until you have reached the goal of completing time-consuming jobs in half the time now spent on them.

4.   Think of yourself as a supervisor evaluating the performance of the workers under you. What clues would you look for to identify individuals who are orderly and organized?

5.   You ride the bus to work. The schedule allows you to arrive either 25 minutes early or three minutes late. What would you do?

6.   Imagine that you are working in a situation where just as you are assigned to do three different jobs—all to be done right away—a critical piece of equipment breaks down. How would you handle such a crisis?

7.   You are assigned to a new job in the accounting department. You are told that the chief accountant, your supervisor, is a perfectionist. What implications does this information have for you? How might you go about learning what standards of performance are expected of you?

8.   In some employment situations you may find yourself confronted with a choice between speed and accuracy. For example, if you check each column of figures four times, your accuracy will be high but you will accomplish only half as much as you would if you checked each column only once. How do you decide on the right balance between speed and accuracy? What circumstances might indicate that extreme accuracy is worth whatever time it takes? What circumstances might indicate that you should sacrifice accuracy to gain speed?

Case Problems

1.   Job or Career?

Laura Montefiero is a salesperson in the clothing department of a department store. The sales staff in the store is paid a weekly salary. No commission is paid for the amount of goods sold.

Laura is very industrious and is usually the first to greet a customer. After serving her customers, Laura returns the clothing to the racks. She then keeps busy arranging merchandise or studying new items that have been recently put in stock. She is always pleasant and courteous.

Dale Salizar, who works with her, tells Laura she is foolish to work so hard when she receives no extra pay. Laura knows that Dale's attitude is characteristic of the feeling of many of the members of the sales force.

1. Is it profitable for Laura to work as she does?
2. Do you feel that Laura may be rewarded for her work attitudes?
3. If Laura does not receive a promotion, can you think of any advantages her attitude would have?
4. Why do you think the other clerks feel as they do about their work?
5. If you were in charge of Laura's department, how would you handle this situation of indifference on the part of some of the sales personnel?

2.   Take Up the Slack.

Martin Brady and Marian Stuart are employed as billing clerks by a merchandising firm. When Martin is asked for certain invoices, he has to rummage through his files before he can find them. He does, however, make out all invoices neatly and accurately. Marian, who occupies the next desk and does the same kind of work, uses a system. She makes notations about invoices that cannot be completed at once and is constantly trying to find shortcuts and timesaving devices.

Martin is always joking with Marian about the latter's "efficiency." Martin tells Marian that she really does not produce more work than he does. However, Marian is promoted to the bookkeeping department to a position that has more responsibility. Martin believes that favoritism is being shown.

1. What businesslike attitudes does Marian show that she possesses?
2. In what ways does Martin show he is not businesslike?

3.   Cluttered Desk.

Jasper Matsura has a basket on his desk marked for incoming work. He has asked his supervisor several times to place any work for his attention in this basket, since his desk tends to get cluttered because of his many interruptions through the day. Nevertheless, his supervisor repeatedly comes in asking for work that Jasper has never seen. When he looks through the accumulated piles of paper on his desk, Jasper finds the requested items.

1. Do you think Jasper has handled the problem correctly? Why or why not?
2. Can you think of another way of handling the problem?

4. Future Dividends.

Ted Tyler was employed as one of two bookkeepers in a small manufacturing concern. Midge Christopher was the manager of the accounting department. Ted found that he could work much faster and more accurately than his fellow employee. He thus had time to spend in doing extra work or in helping the other bookkeeper. Things seemed to go just as well, however, if he took more time with his own tasks. He worked more slowly, therefore, so he would not have to do anything extra.

At the end of the year some special reports and records had to be prepared. Henry Mack was employed as an extra bookkeeper for one month. Although his work was temporary, Henry was interested in the job and worked as hard as he could, doing exceptionally well. At the end of the month, when Henry was scheduled to leave, Midge became ill and had to resign. Midge recommended that Henry be given her vacated post as department manger. This was done.

1. Do you feel Midge was justified in overlooking Ted's seniority in the firm?
2. Do you think Ted had any claim on the position as department manager?
3. In working slowly, what impression did Ted give Midge as to his ability?
4. If Ted had worked more efficiently and then spent the extra time in helping the other bookkeeper, would this have gone unnoticed?

5. Who Is Responsible?

Claire Baker usually proofreads all letters after she transcribes them. Her employer dictated several letters at 4:15 p.m., and because Claire was in a hurry to leave, she mailed these letters without proofreading them. In one letter that asked for the payment of a past-due account of $50, she typed the amount as $40. A prompt reply was received with a check for $40 in full payment of the account. Claire's employer insisted that she make good the difference. Claire agreed, but she thought the demand was very unfair.

1. Who is responsible for errors of this type, the business or the employees who make them?
2. What is the rule when cashiers make mistakes in giving change?
3. Why does business insist on accurate records where money is involved?
4. What opinion might the customer who paid $40 have of the firm?

6.   Quotas at Work.

Some companies set work production quotas for their employees to meet. At times, these quotas may be met by working less time than the normal working day. Or it may be possible to meet the quotas by working extra hard for a few hours only.

1. If you could meet your quota in just six hours (of an eight-hour day), should you just waste time the other two hours?
2. Do you think production quotas are fair:
   a. To employers?
   b. To employees?
3. Should you improve your job performance if you are already meeting your quota? Why or why not?

Chapter 8
Working with others

Conrad had been employed as a dispatcher for a trucking company for two years. He did his job efficiently. He was conscientious and hardworking. However, at times his co-workers and supervisors found him to be "uncooperative," "a loner," and "unable to fit in." After being passed over for a promotion he thought he had earned, Conrad decided to ask his most trusted co-worker, Madeline, to help him understand why he was not selected. In a tactful and kind way, Madeline outlined some suggestions about how Conrad should behave to improve his image as a cooperative member of the working team. If you were in Madeline's position, what suggestions would you offer to help Conrad with his problem?

Learn to Cooperate

In this age of competition, the ability to cooperate—to work smoothly with others—is in danger of becoming a lost art. But cooperation is like a bank account. It is an investment that may not pay immediate dividends. Yet, if deposits are made, the dividends will eventually become both frequent and of a high rate. Like a bank account, too, cooperation may demand the sacrifice of immediate conveniences for later reward.

125

Illus. 8–1. Cooperation: Learn to Work with Others

You must earn the reputation for cooperation. You will earn it by thinking, not of your immediate comfort, but of the ultimate welfare of your firm and your customers. Cooperation is actually an expression of self-interest and unselfishness. It demands that you adjust your immediate pleasure to the best interests of others. Yet the reward for immediate sacrifices is a reputation for cooperation which will contribute to your success.

Cooperation may be a simple little act of sharing your materials or equipment with a co-worker. It may mean helping to cover the territory of another salesperson who is unable to do it alone. It may mean willingness to go out of your way to help a customer or co-worker. It may mean holding back when you want to disagree, being a good sport when you have lost a sale, or showing tolerance in listening to the ideas of others when your own ideas seem superior.

In almost any career you might choose, there will be many occasions when you will be expected to cooperate. These occasions include keeping your workplace and belongings neat and tidy, assuming additional duties and assignments without complaint, working overtime when there is a need, and offering your services even when you are not obligated to do so. You should surrender your own ideas if they do not fit in with the policy of the organization. Tell others of devices that may help them and show unselfishness whenever you can. You should pass on your ideas and the results of your own experiences to others. Listen when others try to help you with their ideas and the results of their experiences. Work harmoniously with others to advance the interests of the organization.

Another way of cooperating is by being on time for appointments. You should observe all of the working rules of the firm and work cheerfully with the fellow employee who has been promoted. Go out of your way to help those who have not yet adjusted to their work. Keeping your reports up to date and turning them in on time is one simple but very effective way of cooperating that is greatly appreciated by managers and supervisors.

Cooperate in maintaining good human relations. Do not criticize the business that employs you, your supervisors, or your co-workers. If you possess business information that should be kept secret, then keep it to yourself. Be willing to take your share of the blame when things go wrong. Show consideration

Illus. 8–2. Learn the art of cooperation.

The Cincinnati Gas & Electric Co.

for others by feeling no resentment when you are called on to do extra work caused by the error of another worker. But try not to create extra work because of your own errors. You can see that the trait of cooperation covers a lot of territory.

Don't Take Advantage of Co-Workers

Sometimes you may have to ask a co-worker to assume some of your responsibilities, but you should never take advantage of another or shirk your own work. When you do ask for help, you should speak well of the person who helps you. If you are cooperative, you should not call attention to the faults or errors of others unless you are their supervisor and your work requires you to evaluate their performance. Even if criticism is part of your work, you will show more cooperation if you point out inefficiencies in an impersonal, constructive way. Your cooperation will encourage the cooperative spirit in others.

Learn How and When to Speak Up

If you are cooperative, you can still express your ideas by making suggestions when you feel they should be made. You must use your good judgment in deciding when you should speak and when you should keep silent. There may be some cases you should protest, but you should also listen to the ideas of your supervisors and your customers. If a decision is made and your ideas have been overruled, you must abide by the decision in a cheerful manner. There are times when a frank discussion may be required, but there are also times for cooperative submission to your firm or your customer.

So much depends on speaking—when to speak, when not to speak, what to say, and what not to say—when working for advancement. It is true that sometimes silence is golden. A beginning worker, for example, should be slow to suggest changes in working procedures. Before you make such suggestions, you should study the reasons for the present processes. You might learn from such study why your changes would not be practical at the moment. Suggesting changes just to prove you are alert and up to date is a practice that can only be detrimental to you.

Silence really is golden when you are tempted to criticize another worker or your employer. Idle criticism will only earn you a reputation for being a troublemaker. Oftentimes, too, when you know the reasons for a person's actions, you will recognize that your intended criticism is undeserved. If you do decide to say something critical, it should be said *to* the person involved and all your critical comments should be presented in a kind and tactful manner.

Think Before You Speak Up

There may be times when you have constructive suggestions to make. The first rule is to learn when and where you should express your views regarding the firm, your office, a particular job process, or a decision. Until you can learn the appropriate timing for such expressions, you should say nothing. Even when you know the right time and place for stating your views, you should do so concisely. Come directly to the point. If explanations are essential, organize them in logical form. It may be that your employers will welcome your suggestions. If, however, you find that your supervisors have different ideas on the subject, you must abide by their decision. You must never argue or refuse to cooperate.

Your Position on the Team

Teamwork in a business is founded on cooperation. Unless every member of the force practices it, there will be a lack of unity of purpose and the final results are likely to be ruinous. As a beginning worker, you must first cooperate by being loyal to the business that employs you. Demonstrate your loyalty by following the suggestions and directions of your supervisor willingly and enthusiastically. Abide by their decisions because they are made with the welfare of the entire organization in mind.

Think of yourself as playing a certain position on your business' team. You may be keeping records. If you are, make sure that these records are accurate and thoroughly checked. If you are a shipping clerk, see that your position is filled perfectly; see that there is no slipup in your part of the team play. If you write the first draft of a report, check the information that goes into the report. Do your very best to see that the report is written as well as you can do it. But remember, like the player in a football game who throws a forward pass, you pass your part of the report to the person, perhaps your supervisor, who is going to write or dictate the final draft. Your supervisor will make the touchdown. You will be the team member who makes it possible for someone else to catch the ball and carry it over the line. You can see why, as a worker, you *must* understand why people behave as they do. Facts and figures may be supplied by machines, but people still make the business enterprise go— or break down. One person can create enough friction to make it break down. You must make sure that *you* are not a behavior problem, but you must also learn to understand others when they are.

Don't Panic—Use Your Head

As a successful worker, first of all, you must learn to follow the motto THINK. You should not let your feelings, your emotions, tell you what to do. But even the best of us cannot hope to be 100 percent objective—even part of the time. There is a good possibility that we do things, and say things, for unconscious reasons. The thing we must do is be on our guard for this possibility. If we are promoted to a new and difficult job, for example, we may find ourselves in a state of panic. If you should find yourself in this position, don't expect to find sensible reasons for your fears. They may be caused by an excessive desire to be perfect. Thus, you may be afraid of failure and not afraid of the job. The cure for your panic may lie in telling yourself that mistakes will almost surely occur at first. The expected, you see, is not so frightening as the unexpected, and you may find your fears disappearing.

Don't Make Hasty Judgments

An understanding of the possible reasons for behavior will keep you from hasty judgments of others. If the person at the desk next to yours takes offense at everything you say, don't stop speaking altogether. It may be that your co-worker is extremely insecure. This person may want to succeed just as much as you do but may feel inferior to the other workers. Such a person may have no idea how to seek help for real or imagined inadequacies. You can help by providing reassurance now and then.

Sometimes unattractive personality traits cover up a tendency that is their exact opposite. Thus, the braggart may be doubtful of self-worth; the person who laughs too much may actually be shy; the excessively sweet person may be covering up a real dislike of people.

You have read in Chapter One about the basic needs that are common to all of us. It will help you to understand your co-workers and supervisors if you review what you have read. Everyone has these same needs. You employer may seem to be the ultimate in success to you, yet may feel completely unappreciated. In fact, the higher you climb the ladder of success, the more lonely you may become. It will help you and your firm if you take the initiative in the friendly greeting, the approving word. No one gets too much appreciation. If you are able to show your appreciation of others, you can make a good start in building a better psychological climate around you.

If you are committed to a greater understanding of others, the next step is to keep from being a behavior problem yourself. It is better to be positive, to be cheerful. Now, let's talk about how you can understand, get along with, and even help others to fit in as members of a working team.

Understand and Use Group Psychology

In almost every workplace there are at least two people, and two people make a group. If you work now, or plan to work someday, you must learn as much as you can about the psychology of groups, what makes *them* tick. How does our group behavior differ from our individual behavior? Why is it so important?

Group behavior is important because whatever you do affects the way someone else in your group feels. When your actions make others feel positively toward you and toward the

Illus. 8–3. Use group psychology when dealing with others.

group, they are helped to do a more effective job. When your actions cause friction and bad feelings in the group members, they will be held back from doing their best work. Thus, your actions will diminish the effectiveness of your group. The problem, then, is to work on yourself, to create the kind of person who brings out the best in people in the group, not one who contributes to the problem that so often exists when people work closely together.

Help The Problem Co-Worker

Even if you personally do not create problems in your group, do you do anything to *help* those who do, group members who drive everyone else up the wall with personal insecurities, negativism, or closed minds? There are two things you can do to help the problem person in your group. First, you can tell about some problem you had when you first joined the group. (Most of us go through an adjustment period when first joining any kind of work or social group.) You can go to the difficult group member and tell what a hard time you had in adjusting to so many different personalities. You can tell how inferior you felt, when everyone else seemed to be so much more competent than you. This is one sure way to help the difficult group member open up to you, to tell you some of the troubles experienced with the group and thus make them less troublesome. The second thing you can do is comment favorably on something the other person has said or done in the group, something that made the work go more smoothly, that helped get things done. If you do this, you will be working to make the group a real one, because real groups are made up of real people. By showing another person the real you, you help that person become more real, too.

The theory behind changing a group so that it works better is called *shaping*. If you can get some of your friends to help you shape the difficult group member, you can accomplish some remarkable results. Shaping means that you pay no attention to the irritating things the group member does, but you give reward or praise for the things said and done that are helpful. Most of the difficulties people have when they become a part of a group are caused by lack of confidence. Praise is a good confidence builder.

The first step, though, is to be a real person yourself. You must be willing to feel and express real feelings. If someone says something to you that makes you feel happy, say so. Say, "That makes me feel wonderful!" If someone says something to you that hurts you, you will be a real person if you can say, "I wish you wouldn't tease me about that. It's something I'm kind of sensitive about." If you say something like this in a straightforward manner, without whining or accusing, you will show the other person a part of the real you. You will remove part of your mask and, in most cases, the other person will respond in the same way. Of course, such statements are hard to make. It is much easier to sulk, to go away, to refuse to talk to the other person. But these actions do nothing but make matters worse between you and the other person. Every bad relationship in a group hurts the group as a whole and makes it less effective in getting things done.

When you want to effect a change in your co-workers, you must proceed indirectly. You cannot call all of your fellow workers together and say, "Look, let's all be real. Let's all try to accept one another." When you do something like this, the rest of the group will wonder what you are after. People do not like to be forced to do things—even if they are for their own good. Shaping works best when the technique begins with you. When you are more real in dealing with your co-workers, that realness becomes contagious. Some of your fellow workers will catch realness from you. Someone else will catch realness from your fellow workers. In an organization where everyone is real, no one needs to wear a mask to cover one's real self. Work no longer seems like work in such an organization. It becomes a very pleasant activity.

How To Talk With Complainers

As you work at the role of shaping others with whom you work, you may have one human relations problem you could do nicely without. You may be the kind of person to whom everyone complains. It is a compliment when others come to you with their troubles, but you'll be tempted to minimize the other person's troubles by saying, "Don't take everything so hard." Such remarks are not appreciated by the complainer who now has something else to complain about—your heartless attitude. One technique has proved to be effective. You merely repeat what has been said to you, but in different words. If a co-worker comes to you and says, "I hate that Mr. Doerle! Just because he's the supervisor doesn't give him the right to treat me like dirt!" you answer, "I can tell Mr. Doerle has made you angry." Statements of this kind help the complainer to begin to calm down. What this technique amounts to is putting the other person's feelings into words. By doing this, you say to the other person that you understand the feelings behind the complaint. You do not condone this violent outburst, but you understand.

This method of reflecting back (a sort of mirror image) of what the other person says was developed by counseling psychologists. It is called the *nondirective approach*. The result of this method of communicating with complainers is that such a device eliminates the so-human tendency to give advice, to preach, or to defend yourself against an implied criticism. The nondirective method, on the other hand, seems to draw out some of the negative feelings and makes it possible for the speaker to pause, take stock of the situation, and think it through.

The same technique is especially effective when the angry person is aiming that anger at you. The same kind of response is the best one. When a co-worker yells at you, "How can you be so clumsy!" you answer calmly, "I don't know. I just seem to be a bit careless at times. I'm sorry." Admitting your own faults to the accuser is almost guaranteed to eliminate the anger in the accuser. The only problem is that you must keep all traces of sarcasm from your voice as you give your calm reply. You see, bad feelings and conflict between people don't just happen, they are caused. Without knowing it, you may be part of the cause. If you can take the giant step of admitting your part of the cause of the trouble, you will help the other person take an equally hard step of admitting to a share of the blame.

Every working group has its stock characters. These may be recognizable at once, or they may be hiding behind a front that is entirely different from the real person. This fact is one reason why you should take your time in joining one of the many groups you will encounter. The secret of a successful entrance into a new employment situation is to be pleasant with everyone. Say "Good morning" to the janitor, the president, and everyone else.

Don't React to Characters in the Group

Every group seems to have a grouch. A beginner may become upset, but remember, the grouch is not mad at you. There may be several reasons for this display of crankiness: home life, finances, or responsibilities at work. If you are pleasant and sympathetic, if you refuse to take the grouch's complaining personally, you may make such a person become less of a grouch.

What about the bossy "nonboss"? There is usually one around. This person criticizes everything you do (and everything others do, too). Remember that bossy people are mainly dissatisfied with themselves. Calling attention to the faults of others is just a way of easing up on this self-dissatisfaction. Pay no attention to the bossy person who is your co-worker. If such a person *is* your boss, however, you will help by paying careful attention to detail and by following directions as accurately as you can.

The complainer is more dangerous than other characters because complaining is highly contagious. The best thing you can do is politely avoid the complainer. Trying to counter complaints with cheerful, positive statements is useless because the complainer is interested only in gloom. Whatever you do, don't let the complainer influence your thinking so that you become a complainer, too.

Another dangerous character is the tattletale. You can recognize a tattletale by the stories told you about other employees. No matter what the provocation, even repeating what one of the employees said about you, don't retaliate. A tattletale will go back to this person and repeat what you have said. Gossip is unwise at any time, but gossip with a tattletale is positively dangerous. When such a person starts telling you some tale about another person, be polite but firm. Suddenly remember a pressing engagement. There are plenty of your co-workers who will listen, unfortunately. The tattletale will leave you alone if you refuse to listen.

Don't Become a Character Yourself

There is one character that you may become—the favorite employee. Try to keep such a situation from developing if you can. If, in spite of your efforts, the employer seems to favor you, do everything you can to stay on good terms with the other workers. You must never try to capitalize on such favoritism. Even though your employer may call *you* by your first name, do not use your employer's first name. You will have everything to gain and nothing to lose if your treat all supervisors with "distance"—that slight formality that indicates respect.

Another character you must not assume is that of the arguer. It is possible to avoid unnecessary arguments; it takes only two ingredients, relaxation and patience. If someone makes a controversial statement, relax. Feel your muscles go limp. Then wait and listen until you have heard the whole story. Many arguments are merely the result of not letting the other person finish. Decide to say nothing until your "opponent" has talked for at least three minutes. By that time, particularly if you are relaxed, you will find yourself much less likely to say something rash, something that might hurt the other person's feelings.

Service With A Smile

Everything that is done in one department is usually of service to some other department. Records are kept, papers are filed, plans are made, and products are produced, all to serve the company as a whole. Any worker, then, must be service conscious. You must be willing to do all in your power to make the company run smoothly. To fit, you must be willing to serve. The typical workplace is no place for the temperamental person.

To recognize the importance of a service attitude, imagine that you are a member of a "bucket brigade" engaged in putting out a fire. A long line of people pass the buckets of water along the line from the stream at one end to the fire at the other. Suppose you drop the bucket when it gets to you? What will happen to the group effort? This is how important each member of the working group can be.

Questions and Projects

1. Few of us could live happily without friends. Try the following steps in winning new friends:

    a. Step One: All day Monday smile at those you meet at school or at work. Praise at least one person you greet.

b. Step Two: On Tuesday relay a kind or encouraging word to every close associate you talk to during the day.

c. Step Three: On Wednesday seek out someone in need of a friend and invite that person to do something with you.

d. Step Four: On Thursday choose a stranger to talk with, dicussing only that person's affairs—not yours.

e. Step Five: On Friday write a friendly letter to someone.

Evaluate the experience of the week. Do you feel more friendly with someone? Has anyone made friendly overtures to you?

2. Assume you have been promoted to supervisor. One of the people with whom you formerly worked is now working under you. Kay is habitually late for work; she is doing a good job otherwise. It is your duty to talk to Kay about her tardiness. What will you say to Kay? Write down your exact words.

3. Choose someone in your place of business who seems aloof and with whom you do not ordinarily talk. Then deliberately start a conversation with that person. What opening remark did you use? How did the conversation go? If your opening statement was not successful, can you see why? What other statements do you think might have been better?

4. The way to avoid arguments is to *relax* and wait for the whole story. The next time you are tempted to argue with someone, say nothing. Just wait and listen. Write down the result of your experience. Did you accomplish anything? Do you feel this is a helpful solution for you?

5. You have been asked to show a new employee around the office. As you start back to your floor, you have an opportunity for conversation. You know the new employee is interested in sports. How would you start the conversation?

6. Think of at least one situation where you work with other people and could be more cooperative. Describe the situation and how you will go about being more cooperative.

7. Humorous stories, particularly if they are brief, add interest and emphasize certain points of view in a conversation. Go through some magazines and collect five stories that you could use in ordinary conversation in your place of employment.

Case Problems

1. To Screen or Not to Screen.

Mr. O'Rourke, your supervisor, comes in from lunch and tells you that he does not want to be disturbed for any reason. He must finish up a complicated report that must be ready for a board meeting at 2 p.m. He tells you to take care of all telephone calls. It is now 1 p.m.

a. You are extremely busy typing the completed section of the report. At 1:15 the telephone rings. When you answer, giving your name and position, the voice says, "Put me on to Pat, will you?" You answer that Mr. O'Rourke cannot be disturbed until four o'clock because of an important meeting. The voice says, "Just tell him it's Lee from Miami. He'll be glad to talk to me." What will you say now?

b. At 1:30 the telephone rings again. The voice is that of Mr. O'Rourke's son. He is extremely agitated and explains that he is calling from a public telephone. He has locked his keys in the car and wants Mr. O'Rourke to bring the spare set to 4879 Collette Drive to unlock the car. Collette Drive is five miles from your office. What do you do?

c. One of your friends, Mary Jane, rings at 1:45 to tell you some important plans about the dinner she is giving this evening. Mary Jane talks fast and is hard to interrupt. What will you say or do?

d. The telephone rings at 1:50. It is Richard Van Der Berghe, the production manager. He says, "Put me on to your boss right now. One of my workers, Beth Richards, has been injured. She's unconscious. Hurry! It's an emergency!" What will you say or do?

2. Constructive Criticism.

Dan O'Riley has the common habit of saying "You know" three or four times in every conversation. In fact, he sometimes repeats this meaningless phrase twice in one sentence. Peter Neerings, who works at the next desk with Dan in the credit department of a large firm, has noticed how Dan's repetition of the phrase annoys their supervisor. Peter decides to mention the matter to Dan. He tells Dan, however, that the mannerism annoys him—rather than mentioning the supervisor. Dan is hurt by the criticism but asks Peter what he can do to break the habit, since he is not aware the he repeats the phrase at all.

1. Assuming you are Peter, can you make any suggestions to Dan to help him break this habit?

2. What do you think of Peter's assuming sole responsibility instead of bringing in the supervisor's name?
3. Can you think of a tactful way of bringing up this matter to avoid hurting Dan's feelings?

3. No Personal Calls.

Ruth McDonald is busy with her work when she receives a personal telephone call from her friend, Harriet. Harriet wants to find out about a weekend trip that is being planned. Harriet is working at her first job; Ruth knows Harriet does not realize that the office is no place for personal calls. Ruth doesn't want to hurt Harriet's feelings, so she tries to be tactful. Finally, she says, "Harriet, I must go now. Mrs. Maxwell is buzzing me. See you Friday."

1. Do you think Harriet was made aware that she should not call Ruth during office hours?
2. Should Ruth have been more honest with Harriet so she would understand how to behave in the future?
3. Can you think of a tactful way that Ruth could have informed Harriet of the general rule regarding personal telephone calls during business hours?

4. Reducing Resistance to Change.

One of your duties as the newly appointed assistant purchasing agent is the supervision of the stock room. In charge of the stock room is Mr. Black, who has been with the company for thirty years. It is he who devised and installed the system of records used in the stock room. This sytem is now out of date, clumsy, and too elaborate.

A major item of concern is how to get Mr. Black's cooperation in making the change from the old system of records to one that is more efficient.

1. How will you win the confidence of Mr. Black?
2. Write down the opening statement you will make when you bring up the matter of installing a new record system for the first time.
3. Assuming that you win Mr. Black's cooperation, what will you say when Mr. Black makes a suggestion that you feel is not a good one? Give your conversation in detail.
4. The new system is now ready to be installed. What will you say to Mr. Black to help get the system off to a good start?

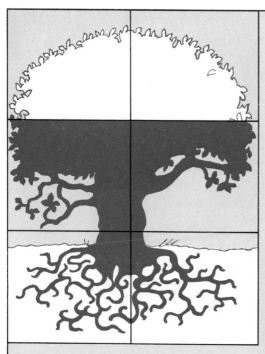

PART FOUR
Coping

Chapter 9
Coping with conflict

"I love humanity. It's people I can't stand." This statement by cartoon character Charlie Brown expresses how many of us feel.

In the abstract, humanity is fine. You love humanity. But there are those awful *people* cluttering up your life: your co-workers, your supervisor, the supervisor's boss. In addition to these problems, however, you will very likely have the same kinds of difficulties with the people in your personal life. There will never be an end to problems with people, but you can arm yourself with a helpful way of handling the ones that come up in your life.

Brush Up Your Human Relations Skills

Garth Larsen was a straight "A" student in his accounting classes at the community college where he completed a mid-management training program. But after six months on his first job as a junior accountant with a large company, Garth was dismissed. His record of performance ratings indicated that he had always done his assigned work exceptionally well. Why did Garth lose his job? Some of the last entries in his personnel file were: "Does not respond to constructive criticism." "Seems to aggravate fellow workers." "Emotionally immature." "Would rather argue than listen." Is Garth's case unusual? How might he have avoided this crisis in his career?

Illus. 9–1. Conflict: Arm Yourself with Skills to Deal with Problems

Success is 90 percent personality. Just what does that statement mean? Does it mean that skill, knowledge, and ability are valueless? No. The statement means that you need all three to *get* the job in the first place. Keeping that job, however, calls for another ingredient. You must be able to get along with other people. The 90 percent figure, by the way, comes from a study that surveyed the reasons why clerical workers *lost* their jobs. In this survey it was found that 90 percent of the reasons given for job dismissal were personal ones. In other words, problems involving conflict with other people may cause you to lose your job, even though you have skill, knowledge, and ability.

Fit in and Get Along

The way you get along with your co-workers will have much to do with your job success and promotional chances. One important factor is your ability to be friendly with everyone without becoming involved in feuds. It is wise to remain somewhat impersonal and detached at first, until you become more familiar with the firm. Be slow to confide in others. Be a listener instead of a confider. Keep the confidences of others, and keep your own confidences to yourself.

Be willing to help others on occasion, but do not permit yourself to be exploited. In every business there are workers who try to find someone to do their work for them. Becoming a party to this sort of thing merely encourages irresponsibility in others.

Learn To Be Tactful

Webster's New Collegiate Dictionary states that tact is "a keen sense of what to do or say in order to maintain good relations with others or avoid offense." It is a sixth sense that makes us aware of what would be fitting to do or say at a given moment. It puts us in the other person's shoes. If you are tactful, you will make life infinitely easier for yourself and those around you. Tact involves understanding the other person's needs and wishes.

The following list of such situations should be studied carefully. Describe how you would use tact in each of them.

Illus. 9–2. Learn to be tactful when faced with conflict.

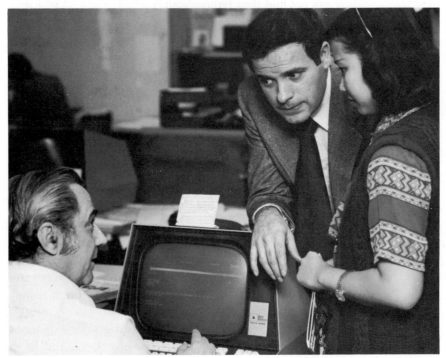

Copyright *RCA Global Communications, Inc.*

1. Maintaining any business relationship on an impersonal basis.
2. Handling a telephone communication in order to facilitate the smooth operation of the business situation involved.
3. Dismissing unwanted callers.
4. Making visitors feel at ease if they are kept waiting.
5. Answering questions about the business that are asked by outsiders.
6. Avoiding being pumped by outsiders for information about the business.
7. Ascertaining a caller's business before disturbing your employer.
8. Giving callers the impression that, no matter how trifling the interview may be, your employer will be glad to see them if possible.
9. Knowing when and how to enter your employer's office or to withdraw from it.
10. Suggesting improvements to be made, equipment to be installed, and supplies to be furnished.
11. Asking for a promotion or a raise.
12. Responding pleasantly and courteously when you have been spoken to in a rude manner.
13. Putting people at ease.
14. Taking care of an unpleasant situation so that those involved will be spared embarrassment.

15. Making necessary criticisms of other people in such a way that you will not hurt their feelings unduly.
16. Being considerate of subordinates.
17. Complimenting a fellow worker on a job well done.
18. Dealing with adverse criticism. Thank the critic and show an eagerness to improve.
19. Settling a difference of opinion among fellow employees.
20. Disagreeing with another without being disagreeable.
21. Remembering the names of people for whom and with whom you work.
22. Sending a sales representative away satisfied with the interview, though no sale has been made.
23. Dealing with an angry customer.
24. Collecting an account.
25. Explaining to a customer, without losing the business of that customer, why an article cannot be returned.

You Can't Change Others with Criticism

The most frustrating aspect of human relations is discovered when you try to change someone else. Your best friend, Ted, mispronounces words. So, with the best intentions, you correct him. Is your friend grateful? Does he thank you for your interest in his self-improvement campaign? No, he is not grateful and he does not thank you. He resents your meddling, and he resents it deeply. Furthermore, just to show you who is boss, he does not improve.

Use Behavior Modification

Using behavior modification to change the actions of others is simple. It involves what psychologists call *reinforcement*. This is how it works. If the desired behavior shows up in the other person, you give praise. If the kind of behavior you dislike is shown, you walk away; you say nothing; you ignore it. The use of reinforcement is so simple, really, that you may not believe that it works. Before you decide, though, try this plan with someone who aggravates you. For example, you have a friend who constantly complains. While you like the friend, this habit of complaining is annoying to you. You decide to try behavior modification. Every time the friend complains, criticizes, finds fault, you make some excuse and leave. If this action seems too drastic, just look away and seem to be paying no attention.

On the other hand, when the friend says something positive, or expresses an interest in you or in other people in a positive way, you listen; you make positive comments; you praise your friend for a helpful attitude.

When you are alone, write down how many negative comments the friend made before you started your plan. Then keep track of the negative comments made each time you use reinforcement to bring about more positive comments. You may be surprised to find that before too many sessions have passed, your friend will have become less negative, less critical.

You may need help, at first, avoiding criticism and, in its place, giving praise. (A great many people find it hard to give praise to others.) Practice using the following words and phrases:

Good	I'm pleased with that
That's right	Great
Exactly	I like that
Good job	That's interesting

Illus. 9–3. Criticize work or actions rather than the person.

Photo by Cheryl Walsh Bellville, Courtesy of The St. Paul Companies, Inc.

Another thing: If you find that you *must* be critical of someone, make sure you criticize the work or action—not the person. And try to be tactful. You can disapprove of what a person does without being critical of the person.

You are now armed with two weapons for making things happen. You are learning to be tactful and you are using behavior modification to change others. Now you are ready to tackle the third weapon: learning how to make decisions. What a lot of time we could save if we could just make decisions quickly. We have a decision to make; we debate endlessly; we ask advice from friends and relatives, all of whom give us conflicting replies; we decide to wait until the next day to make up our minds— only to have the whole process repeated. A way out of this dilemma is available. The first step is to decide whether the decision is a major or a minor one. If the decision is which movie to see or which outfit to wear, we flip a coin—and abide by the decision. If the decision is a major one, however, one that involves important stakes, we need another method.

Decisions Involving People

For several weeks Marie Hogan, Credit Union manager, had been vaguely aware that something was seriously wrong. Members (the "customers" of a credit union) had complained on several occasions recently. All the complaints had to do with employees being rude, careless, or unconcerned about member problems. On one occasion Marie overheard a conversation in which one employee severely reprimanded a younger co-worker for not doing something at once. It was obvious that morale was low and that the Credit Union was losing business because of member dissatisfaction with the services being provided and the negative attitudes of the employees. What should Marie do in this situation? How might she prepare for making a decision?

A logical way of solving problems with people is one that has been used for many years in science and in business. It is sometimes called the scientific method. We are going to change the method slightly, however, because we are going to use five steps to solve problems with people—in other words, people difficulties. The five steps are answers to the following questions:

(1) What is the problem? (2) What are the facts? (3) What is my overall objective? (4) What are some possible solutions? and (5) Which is the best solution?

What Is the Problem?

The first step in solving a problem is to state it clearly and concisely. This may sound easy, but there is nothing more difficult. You may know something is wrong—but you don't know exactly what. Someone has said that a problem well stated is a problem half solved. How should you state the problem? One way is to ask a question. Care must be taken, however, not to give judgments in the statement of the problem. Be objective; do not favor anyone. Just state the problem in specific terms.

For example, assume that you have been working in a shipping and receiving department for two years. The supervisor, John Phillips, suddenly retires because of ill health and you are promoted to his position over the head of Joan Tyler, a veteran of the company and the person who expected to be made supervisor. Joan is polite to you, but noncooperative. She does her job and that's all. Worse still, the other 23 workers in the division are beginning to take sides. How would you state this problem? It is *not*: Why should Joan Tyler act like this? It is *not*: Should a person be promoted over the heads of those who have been in the firm longer? The problem is concerned with what you should do about the situation as it is. It could, of course, be stated in more than one way, but one possibility is the following: What steps can I take to improve the morale and production of this shipping and receiving department in light of the resentment felt over a newcomer's being made supervisor? You will notice that there is no question of right or wrong in this statement of the problem. Nor is there any attempt at a solution, which should be the last of the steps and not the first. This statement is also objective, another necessary feature.

What Are the Facts?

When you answer the second question, "What are the facts?" you must be careful to write down only facts, not opinions or moral judgments. You must keep out all prejudice, all "oughts" and "shoulds." For instance, it is not a fact if you say Joan Tyler is acting like a spoiled child. A statement of this kind implies a judgment of the facts rather than a statement of them. An objective statement of the same implication would be that Joan Tyler does not cooperate to the extent she did before the promotion. The facts, then, should be stated without emotional coloring.

After you have stated as many real facts as you can that apply to the situation, to the problem you wish to solve, it will be helpful if you will arrange them so that the most important facts—the ones that make a difference in the solution—are at the head of your list.

What Is My Overall Objective?

The third step is the hardest one. Perhaps you have never really thought about your main goal in a particular situation. It really helps, though, if you can force yourself to write down exactly where you want to go, exactly where you are headed.

In the shipping and receiving department problem, for example, your overall objective may be to keep your job. You don't want to be fired. Or your overall objective may be broader: you want to keep your job, bring peace to the department, and place departmental productivity at an even higher level than it was before your promotion. You don't want to resign in favor of Joan Tyler just to have peace restored. By now you can see that thinking the question through logically will help you to decide what your real objective is.

What Are Some Possible Situations?

The fourth step is to write down as many solutions to your problem as you can think of. One method of clearing the way for a good solution is to write down the extreme solutions first. Extreme solutions are seldom the best ones. In our problem, such solutions would be: (1) fire Joan Tyler; (2) resign from your job as supervisor; (3) resign from the company. Now the way is clear to devote your attention to constructive solutions, those which would take into consideration the complex human relation factors involved, yet would be forward-looking in terms of getting the work of the division done well.

What Is the Best Solution?

The last step is to choose the best solution. The best solution will meet the two parts of the following standard: (1) The most important facts in step two must have been taken care of. That is, the best solution must improve the situation as it stands as far as the important elements of the problem are concerned. (2) It must help and not hinder you in reaching your overall objective.

In the problem under discussion, the best solution might have a number of parts. There would be first, the solution in terms of Joan Tyler, the resentful employee. It might be well to ignore her negative attitude and begin to build a better feeling between the two of you. This could begin by asking her (without making too much of it) to take charge of some project. This could be followed by commendation for any good work that she does. The best solution for you, as a new, inexperienced supervisor, would be to give yourself time to grow into the job. One fact of life in any kind of work is that authority cannot be maintained on an equality basis. In other words, there must be some distance between the one in authority and the ones over whom such authority exists. You must not expect to be liked by all of the workers under you. Because you have been chosen by your superiors to do a job, however, you should do all you can to make that job a success. An impersonal attitude toward negative feelings of others, plus a sincere determination to merit your workers' respect, will go a long way toward bringing about the needed change in their attitudes. If you keep your attention on getting the work done, while you are fair and positive toward those who work under you, you should expect the morale of the division to improve in time.

You are now armed with your third weapon for becoming a person who makes things happen. With the five-step decision-making method, you are equipped to solve the problems that come up in every possible line of work—as well as the problems that come up in your personal life. One reason for the success of the five-step method is the mental attitude you must adopt if you are to follow the first three steps. You cannot answer the first three questions (What is the problem? What are the facts? and What is my overall objective?) until you become detached emotionally from the problem. When you can shelve your emotions temporarily and put your Adult self in charge, you may find that the correct decision appears to you before you get to step four. The secret of good decision-making is to use mental judgment rather than the emotional pitfalls of "getting even" or "showing who is boss." Practice in making decisions by the five-step method is one of the best-known ways of putting your Adult self in charge.

Questions and Projects

1. Describe a human relations problem that exists among those of your acquaintance. Go through the five steps given in this chapter, from stating the problem to choosing the best solution. Try to be completely objective. Submit your problem for evaluation.

2. In order to get along with all sorts of customers, you will need intelligence and tact. What would you say:

- a. To an angry customer who says, "I thought you said this material was silk. It's marked synthetic blend." (You made a careless error in stating facts.)
- b. To a trying customer who says, "Why do I have to buy the whole unit? All I need is this one part."
- c. To a customer who runs a large account who says, "I placed this order a month ago. Either fill it or forget it!"

3. The following situations are presented for your decision as to how you would handle them. Write your exact words and the probable replies of the other person.

- a. Your supervisor, Mr. Montesari, is away for a week on business. One of the managers comes in and demands that you call him long distance because of a personal conflict with another manager. You have Mr. Montesari's itinerary, but he asked you not to bother him with ordinary matters, since he plans to be very busy and seldom in one place long enough to take a telephone call. Ms. Nakamura, the assistant to Mr. Montesari, is handling routine matters.
- b. An important sales representative, James Metzner, whose products are used by your company, comes in and asks to see Mr. Montesari.
- c. Mr. Montesari returns from his business trip. The morning has been hectic. He has a board of directors meeting at 10:30. It is now 10:25. He says, "Are those reports ready? Where are the tables I gave you to type? Where did I put those statements? Did you call Karen Olsen, the electrician?" You have taken care of all these details. How will you answer Mr. Montesari?
- d. At noon, just before going to lunch, Mr. Montesari returns from his board of directors meeting in a bad mood. He says, "Where in thunder did you put that letter from Washington? I had it in my briefcase,

but it isn't there now! Can't I keep anything around here without somebody running off with it?" Mr. Montesari had asked you to file the letter just after he came in that morning. What do you do or say?

e. At 3:30 Mr. Montesari is meeting in his office with the two vice-presidents on a serious matter. He told you as he went in to the meeting that he was not to be disturbed. An important client comes in on urgent business, something that cannot wait. What do you do or say?

4. You work as assistant manager in a fast-food service business. How would you cope with the following situations? Write your exact words and describe your actions. Also, indicate how you would expect the other person to respond.

a. It has been a long night. Robin, a high school junior, has made a first job (in the fast-food business) a nightmare for you, the supervisor. Just at closing time Robin spills a pan of french fries on the floor behind the counter.

b. You are taking care of the daily cash accounting and discover two checks, written by the same person, for fifty cents and for eighty-seven cents. You recognize the name on the checks as the same as the name of one of Robin's friends.

c. Two of your best workers, Sally and Chris, get into an argument over who should work the late shift on Saturday night. They have been trading work assignments without your approval, and now Chris feels that Sally is being unfair in refusing to "even things up on the Saturday night marathon." Chris wants to switch assignments again and Sally refuses.

d. You hear a commotion in the dining area. When you check to see what is going on you find three teenagers engaged in an ice-throwing spree, using paper cups and ice from the container behind a counter where customers are not supposed to be. A dozen of your regular customers are cheering them on.

Case Problems

1. Delegating Responsibility.

Jane Heiman was instructed by Mrs. Bishop to obtain some information for the latter to use in making out a report of customers who had overdue accounts. By error Jane added the name of a good customer who had never been in arrears. The customer was approached by the credit collection bureau and became highly indignant, calling the general manager of Mrs. Bishop's company, and threatening to do business elsewhere. The general manager called Mrs. Bishop into the office and reprimanded her. Mrs. Bishop insisted that it was not her fault, that Jane had made the error. The general manager said nothing to Jane, but persisted in blaming Mrs. Bishop.

1. Do you agree or disagree with the general manager?
2. What was Mrs. Bishop's responsibility in the matter?
3. If you delegate some of your responsibility to another, what must you be sure to do?
4. If you are capable of assuming responsibility, what would your reaction be to the reprimand from the general manager?

2. In the Groove.

Neva Garcia, who has been transferred from the central office to one of its branches, finds it difficult to adjust herself to the new methods. She is continually referring to her old position: "Miss Brown wanted all computer printouts set up in this manner," is one of her pet sayings. Some of Neva's ideas are good, and in time she may be able to contribute to the efficiency of the branch's routine. At present, however, she annoys everyone else there. Unless Neva adjusts to the new situation, she is in danger of losing her position.

1. What should Neva's attitude be toward her job?
2. Why is it best for a newcomer to refrain from making suggestions about changes?
3. If Neva's ideas are good, how and when may she present them for consideration?
4. Is there a similarity with this situation and the common practice of saying, "This is the way my teacher in school told us to do this"?

3. Keeping Distance.

Ken Mears has worked for the ABC Company for five years and has just been promoted to office manager. Jane Harrison has been working in the same office for just two weeks. Her job is in the credit and collections department. Jane and Ken were in high school together. At noon on the first day after Ken had accepted his new job, Jane asked Ken to go to lunch as her guest to celebrate the promotion.

1. If you were Ken, what would you say to Jane?
2. What would be the best attitude for Jane to assume toward Ken in the future?
3. What would be the effect on the office force if Ken were to accept?
4. What attitude should Ken have toward all his former co-workers—and Jane?

4. The Difficult Boss.

Mr. Tims, a patent attorney, is struggling to build up his own business. To save money, he hires young and inexperienced office workers. He is demanding and criticizes his employees angrily when they make any mistakes. He constantly reminds them how much work there is to be done and tells them they should work faster. An example of a daily occurrence follows:

Charles, a conscientious beginner, presents a letter to Mr. Tims for his signature in which he has added an undictated comma; the rules of punctuation demanded the change. When Mr. Tims notices this one change in an otherwise perfect letter, he calls Charles to his desk, crosses out the comma, and writes "Retype" in pen across the top of the page. Charles is upset; now he will have to retype the letter when he could have erased the offending comma. Moreover, he feels he was right in his action.

Anne, who is dependable and efficient, has spent several minutes trying to find the correct spelling of a peculiar name in the telephone directory. She finally turns to Charles to see if he has any idea of how to spell it. Before Charles has a chance to reply, Mr. Tims (who has his desk in the same room) looks up and says, "Work on your own projects, people."

Both Charles and Anne find the work interesting, but they feel the only solution to the problem is to resign.

Solve the problem with the five-step method described in Chapter 9.

5. Is the Customer Always Right?

An irate customer enters a plumbing supply store with a faucet that she has purchased from a salesperson who said the faucet would fit her bathroom sink. The customer has obviously installed the faucet incorrectly, thereby ruining the gaskets and scratching the chrome finish. The customer proceeds to vent all her anger on Chris Gallegos, who is taking the regular salesperson's place that day.

1. Is this situation a common happening?
2. If you were Chris, what would you say to the customer? Would you try to handle the situation yourself? Why or why not?
3. Was the customer justified in the complaint?
4. If you had been the customer, how would you have handled the situation?

Chapter 10
Coping with stress

Rick was depressed. It seemed that his work, his social life, hobbies and recreation meant nothing to him. Other people aggravated him more often now than ever before. He found himself lashing out in anger, brooding in frustration, feeling very "down" most of the time. It seemed he was not really interested in anything or anyone—except himself. Rick began to see his friends slipping away. He began to pick up clues that his employer was not supporting him for a promotion he had been hoping for. Finally, it was obvious to Rick that he was his own worst enemy. He asked himself "Is there any way that I can turn my life around?"

Getting Yourself Together

One of the difficulties encountered in growing on the job is that of becoming a whole person—in other words, getting yourself together. In fact, no big step should ever be taken when you feel torn, splintered, not all together. The ideal state, of course, would be to go through life "in one piece." This idea seldom comes about, however, and the newcomer to the job market may feel pulled apart. Well-meaning teachers, friends, relatives, future bosses, all give conflicting advice. Before you can begin to grow, therefore, you must get yourself together, find out who you are, know what you think and feel. In short,

Illus. 10–1. Stress: Use Action in Place of Anxiety to Cope

you must become a real person—not just somebody's daughter, son, wife, husband, employee, or whatever.

To be able to feel deeply the good things of life is a real blessing. Positive emotions make our lives worth living. But what about the negative emotions? What do they do to us? When you are seized with anger, hatred, jealousy, fear, worry, can you handle your usual tasks with efficiency and skill? In most cases, you cannot. The destructive emotions are just that. They destroy peace of mind, well-being, and often physical health. Is there anything we can do to control the destructive emotions? Here are some suggestions.

Don't Fight the Problem

A fallacy in this wilderness of problems with people is the belief held by many that you can talk the problem away. You can say, "This should not be," and all may agree with you; but it still *is*. So, when you are up for promotion and possess all the needed abilities and skills only to have a member of the boss's family get the promotion, don't try to fight the problem. Bosses' families will continue, no doubt, to be promoted. Fighting the problem should be avoided; it will not alter the situation.

What you should do when the other fellow is obviously wrong and you are obviously helpless is to let it go. Chalk this one up to experience. Do something else for awhile, something that is enjoyable for you. Let your resentment out of your system through some kind of positive activity. In almost every language there is a proverb to the effect that we should change what we can change but accept what we cannot change.

Have an Emotional Outlet

An important part of keeping your emotional balance in the working world is having an emotional outlet outside of working hours. Sports provide this outlet for many people, but not everyone enjoys sports. To be effective, your hobby must be one that *you* enjoy. There is no definition of a good hobby. Anything you can lose yourself in is good for you. If you have a

Illus. 10–2.   Find an emotional outlet outside of work to relieve stress.

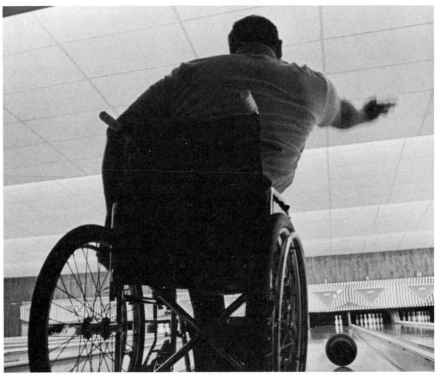

Aetna Life & Casualty Co.

talent, expressing that talent is the best hobby for you. There can be tremendous emotional release in little theatre productions, amateur orchestras and quartets, painting, photography, or writing.

If you feel you have no talent, but have goodwill, you can find just as effective an outlet. Helping the helpless brings great emotional satisfaction. Call the hospitals. Ask if they need someone to read to children. Call the blind centers and ask if readers are needed. In most universities there is a great need for readers for those students who have poor vision. Local rest homes offer unlimited opportunities for bringing happiness to those who feel unwanted.

No matter what your career may offer, you need an outlet that *you* consider rewarding. And don't let someone else tell you that the hobby you have chosen is without value. People's emotions are individual, and only you can make your choice. Choose your emotional outlet and promote your emotional health.

Keep Yourself In a Good Frame of Mind

A part of your human relations skill must go to keeping yourself in a good frame of mind. When you take a new job, you will probably go through periods of discouragement and dissatisfaction. You may receive reprimands, or you may be impatient with your mastery of the new position. When such times of disappointment come, try especially hard to do your job well. Self-discipline means you will not let your productivity respond to the variation in your own feelings. Knowing that there will always be difficult times in any job may help you cope with your problems.

There are cases where employees become indifferent to the demands of their jobs or where they are poorly prepared for the jobs they hold. If this should happen to you and someone in authority should point it out to you, be grateful. You should attempt to find and correct the source of the trouble. In other instances, however, even well-prepared employees with good work habits and good attitudes may feel tense and ill at ease in new positions.

Don't Be Too Sensitive

Psychologists say that many people are too sensitive. If you are sensitive to the point that you feel other people are often sniping at you, criticizing you, or cheating you, you should examine your own feelings. Suspicious people cannot be happy or work easily with others. Self-understanding and self-discipline can frequently relieve this excessive sensitivity and give you a trust in others, enriching all your relationships. Sometimes all you need to do is recognize excessive sensitivity for what it is: self-consciousness or thinking too much about yourself.

Don't Worry About It

Psychologists say that many employees are anxious. Of course, if you are not performing your best work, you may have reason to be anxious. In such a situation, *action*, not anxiety, is required. Whatever is bothering you should be studied and remedied. Work habits and attitudes can be changed by a determination to do so; lack of technical training can be remedied through further education and experience.

When the anxious feeling does not seem to be caused by any actual failure, discovery of the reason may be impossible. There are steps you can take, however. You can do the very best work of which you are capable, not because you want to appear efficient in your employer's eyes, but because *you* want to do well. Second, you can make yourself think of something else every time you begin to worry about yourself. Make it a point to say something cheerful and pleasant to someone else when you feel anxiety coming on.

Talk It Out With Someone

One of the best bits of therapy for excessive anxiety is talking it out with a counselor. Large firms may employ a company psychologist, or they may assign this task to the personnel director. If you can discuss your fears with such a professional, you may be better able to understand your weaknesses and how to overcome them. Or, if professional help is not available to you, talking to a trusted friend, teacher, or co-worker can be very helpful.

Don't Let Fatigue Take Over

Anxiety may manifest itself by worry or by excessive fatigue. Of course, fatigue may be actually merited. You may be getting insufficient sleep; you may be overworking; you may be involved in too many outside activities. If there seems to be no actual physical reason for your fatigue, however, anxiety is probably the cause, and monotony, the symptom. If you do find your work monotonous, you might suggest to your supervisor that you rotate with other workers on repetitive jobs. Another suggestion is to change the way you do your work. One successful device is to time yourself on repetitive tasks, trying to cut down on the time taken while you continue to maintain high accuracy. If you can increase the interest and attention you give your work, you may be able to increase your enthusiasm for it.

Another change of pace that helps fatigue is a complete change of activity outside office hours. If you sit at a desk all day, you will definitely benefit from physical activity after work. Gardening, home maintenance, a sport—anything that makes you use the larger body muscles—will help to give you more pep and energy for your regular work.

Take Your Emotional Temperature

No matter how you have felt about your personality in the past, the important point is how you are doing right now. You see, the trouble with many improvement campaigns is that they go the wrong way. We measure the mistakes we have made, how we have failed. A much more fruitful exercise is to measure how we have succeeded. Furthermore, your personality growth is an individual matter. It won't help you if you pattern your personal qualities after those of someone else. What you need instead is some kind of standard, some indication of your own personal growth.

Fourteen of Maslow's [1] points make up a description of a person who is all together, who is OK, and who feels OK. These fourteen points might be considered your emotional thermometer against which you can measure how you are doing from time to time. Remember, though, that there is no end to personal growth. We will never be totally free from personal faults. No one ever reaches the state of perfection. Still, it will help if we can see measurable improvement over the years. Measure yourself against these standards today; then go through the fourteen points again in six months. See if you have made any progress.

1. You will be able to detect the fake, the phony, the dishonest, and to judge people correctly and efficiently. You will be able to perceive reality and be comfortable with reality. You will not be frightened by the unknown.

2. You will be able to accept. You will be able to accept yourself, accept others, accept nature without thinking about it much one way or another. You will enjoy your physical side without guilt. You will be able to be yourself and you will dislike artificiality in others. What you will feel guilty about are shortcomings that could be improved: laziness, hurting others, prejudice.

3. You will be spontaneous, simple, and natural. Your codes of behavior may be strict, but they will be your own.

---

[1] A. H. Maslow, *Motivation and Personality* (New York: Harper & Row, 1970), pp. 153–180.

You will be ethical, yet your ethics may not be the same as those of the people around you.

4.   You will be problem centered; you won't fight the problem to defend your own ego. You won't spend time worrying about yourself but will do what needs to be done. You will be concerned with the good of people in general, with all of the members of their families in general. You will seem to be above the small things of life, and this will make life easier not only for you, but for all who associate with you.

5.   You will need detachment and privacy. You will like to be alone more than the average person does. You will be able to take personal misfortunes without reacting violently, as the ordinary person does. You may even concentrate so much on the main problem that you earn the "absent-minded professor" title.

6.   You will become independent of your environment; you will be interested in growth rather than in attaining some goal. Less healthy individuals must have people around them; but the self-actualizing person, the person who is concerned with personal growth, may be hampered by the clinging demands of others.

7.   You will have the capacity to appreciate freshly, again and again, the basic goods in life. Any sunset is as beautiful as your first sunset; any flower is of breathtaking loveliness even after you have seen a million flowers. You will derive ecstasy, inspiration, and strength from the basic experiences of life— not from going to a nightclub, or getting a lot of money, or having a good time at a party.

8.   The mystic experience may be fairly common to you. You may experience the feeling of being simultaneously more powerful and more helpless than you ever were before, of great wonder and awe, of the loss of place in time.

9.   You will have a deep sympathy and affection for human beings in general.

10.   You will have a few very close friends.

11.   You will have an unhostile sense of humor. The kind of jokes Lincoln told—mainly on himself—will be the type you like.

12. You will be creative, original, inventive. This does not mean a special creativeness, but rather that you will be creative within the scope of your own natural talents. You will find joy in a new approach to your task.

13. You may not always be a conformist. You will get along with the culture in various ways, but while you will not be rebellious in the adolescent sense, you will resist conformity.

14. You will make some mistakes. You will not be totally free from guilt, sadness, and conflict—because these conditions are normal in our lives today. But you will be able to accept your own blame, pick up the pieces, and go on.

Learn to Control Your Emotions

In order to control any emotion that may be a problem to you—jealousy, worry, fear—you must first identify it, describe it, state what it is. In Chapter 9 you learned to state the problem as the first step in the problem-solving process. You should do the same thing with a destructive emotion: Define the emotion. What is *worry*, for example? You might say that it is a nameless dread for which you can find no real cause.

The next step in your campaign to control destructive emotions is to write down what the emotion does, what its manifestations are. In the case of worry, you might say it causes sleeplessness or, in some cases, sleeping too much; lack of appetite or overeating; headaches; mental blocks; lack of physical coordination; poor memory for facts that you know. Excessive and prolonged worrying may cause you to become depressed.

The third step is to give an example, in your own life or in the life of someone you know, of what the emotion has brought about. This serves as a dramatic object lesson, showing vividly why it is wise to learn to control this emotion. In the case of worry, there is hardly a student anywhere who has not had the experience of worrying over an examination to the point of not being able to think at all. This kind of experience shows the destructiveness of worry better than any number of abstract statements.

The fourth step consists of writing down all of the possible actions that might help to control the destructive emotion. In the case of worry, the list might include the following:

Illus. 10–3. Do something about the cause of your worry.

1. Set aside a certain time of day, or day of the week, for worrying. Then, when a worrisome thought enters your mind, just file it away to be worried about on Thursday!

2. Do something about the cause of the worry. If you worry about finances, start a budget; if about failing a course in school, study an extra half hour a day. This way of controlling emotions is an excellent one because it gets behind the emotion itself to one of its possible causes.

3. Invent some mental process that will automatically take place whenever the tendency to give in to the emotion arises. In the case of anger, you might think of something beautiful— a lovely lake you have seen, the melody of a favorite musical selection, a line from a favorite poem. In the case of worry, one of the best devices is a slogan. Some of these are old, but they are still around because they have proved their effectiveness through the generations. Such slogans as "Take one step at a

time," "Rome was not built in a day," "What will it matter in a thousand years?" might help in the case of worry.

4. Forget the past. This is an important rule in the case of most of the destructive emotions. We get angry at a best friend and rake up old resentments from the past only to find we no longer have a best friend. It is almost impossible to hear someone rebuke us for a past action without retaliating in kind. Too frequently words are spoken that cause wounds that can never be healed. Whatever the emotion you are working on, forget your past failures. The past is gone; nothing can be done about it; so let it go.

5. Do or say something positive in line with the emotion. If you hate someone or dislike someone intensely, the best way to get rid of this emotion is to do something positive, something considerate, for that person. It is almost impossible to dislike someone for whom you have just done a kindness. The magic does not work, however, if you expect *any* kind of reward for your good deed. Don't expect to be thanked. The kindness should be done merely because it is good for *you* to do it. There will be intangible benefits, but don't look for a reward. In fact, the best way to accomplish this is to do something considerate anonymously; this is guaranteed to take the sting of hatred away from that person.

What Emotions Say to Us

Whatever our emotional difficulty—fear, anger, jealousy, hate, worry—there is a reason for its being there. Sometimes the reason is the exact opposite of what the emotion appears to be. It may be the other side of the coin. If you are jealous of someone's affection, for example, this may not mean that you care for the person deeply. It may mean instead that you are insecure about your own worth. You cannot believe that you are worthy of love; therefore, you cling possessively to the person who is closest to you. If you hate someone, this emotion says that you feel unappreciated. You are filled with resentment because your ability, accomplishment, or knowledge have not received recognition, while someone else's have. Then this person has had the nerve to belittle you in some way! It is the belittling that triggers the dislike, but the lack of appreciation is the real cause.

Envy is another resentful emotion, but here we are not sure of our abilities. Perhaps we would like to be brilliant or talented, but feel we are not. The envious emotions say that we are insecure and that we resent this insecurity.

Worry, the kind that has no known cause, comes from hostility that we refuse to admit. That is why it is important that we take a good look at worry and at ourselves. We must admit that we are not perfect, that we may have negative feelings toward those we should love.

What We Should Say to Emotions

No matter what the emotion may be that is making your life miserable, you must not let it have its say. Learn to control it. Listen to what it tells you; then do something to change the situation that brings the emotion about. This means that you should become more lovable instead of being jealous and possessive. It means that you should become more appreciative of the accomplishments of others. Sooner or later someone will, in return, become appreciative of your accomplishments.

Don't waste your life waiting for people to come to you. Take the first step. Then, while you are appreciating the achievements of others, work hard to become an expert at one thing. Many of us try to be musicians, writers, actors, debaters, athletes, and political leaders all at once. No one can succeed in so many different fields. Choose the one activity that gives you the most satisfaction and that you do reasonably well. Then concentrate on that activity. Be willing to start at the bottom. Be willing to work on the team. It will not be long before your worth is recognized.

Questions and Projects

1. Interview an experienced worker in a field you might be interested in for your future employment. Ask the worker to discuss some of the emotional incidents during the first year of employment that were difficult or critical.

2. If you are worried about a test or an interview, how do you cope with your anxiety? Is some fear natural and normal?

3. Have you ever lost your temper or in any other way lost control of your emotions in a working situation? If so, what was the result? Do you see any other way you could have handled the situation? Explain.

4. Think of all the people you know who might be willing and able to talk with you about your emotional problems. Can you identify someone with whom you have a close, trusting relationship—someone you would feel comfortable sharing your innermost feelings with?

5. Think of all the people you know who might think of you as a person with whom they could comfortably discuss personal problems. Are you that kind of person? If so, why? If not, why not?

6. Take your "emotional temperature" using the fourteen points described in this chapter. Write a brief comment with respect to each point, measuring yourself against these standards.

7. What are several tactics you might use to control your emotions when you are under emotional stress? Give examples of each.

8. Think of an incident in your past—preferably more than a month ago—when you were really mad at someone. Write a list of the reasons for your feelings. Be as honest with yourself as you can. Analyze the list, consider the actions you took and the results of your actions. Write the highlights of a different plan of action that might have been better, or less distressing, for yourself and others.

Case Problems

1. Hard, Not Heartless.

Ida Meyerhoffer is feeling low. She has been at work only a week and today Karl Johnson, the assistant manager, spoke to her sharply because she spent half an hour showing clothing to a fussy customer who walked out without making a purchase. Ida is hanging the clothes back on the racks and trying very hard not to show how dark her world has grown because she knows the store is no place for the display of emotions. Sally Walton, the floorwalker, notices Ida and remembers how she felt the first time she had been reprimanded. She decides to say something to Ida to help her feel better.

1. How might Sally Walton help Ida over this episode?
2. Should Karl Johnson speak to his sales personnel as he does?
3. Should Sally Walton tell Ida not to worry about Karl Johnson's reprimands?
4. What constructive suggestions could Sally Walton make?

2. Private Lives.

Maria Perri has recently been divorced. She feels she is a complete failure. She has returned to work at her old job as an advertising copywriter for Specialty Foods, Inc. Maria is a good worker, but she is not adjusting well from her divorce. She spends a good deal of time talking with others about her unhappy marriage; she cries if reprimanded; and she talks on the telephone for about twenty minutes every day during business hours. Vivian Rugerri has tried to be patient with Maria, knowing her capabilities and realizing the difficulties of her personal life. Now, however, she decides to tell Maria that she must be more businesslike in the office.

1. If you were Vivian Rugerri, what would you say first to Maria?
2. Would you give Maria a warning?
3. Do you think Maria should be discharged?
4. What other action could Vivian Rugerri take?

3. Nerves—Your Friend or Your Enemy?

Jim Allison has been working for Corliss Associates, a public relations firm, for three years and has done good work. In his ratings every six months, there is only one negative criticism that can be made. Jim puts too much nervous energy into ordinary jobs; and when one of high pressure comes along, he gets too nervous, works too fast, does work over, and generally does work below his usual standard.

The personnel manager is looking for a private secretary to the head of the firm, Tom Corliss. Tom wants a secretary with energy and initiative, one who can take care of clients while he is away from the office. This is an important factor, as Tom travels a good deal. In looking over the ratings of the people in the office who might be promoted to the job as private secretary, Tom is impressed with Jim's credentials. He scored the highest of any applicant on the intelligence test that is given to everyone who is considered for employment; his skills are excellent; he is a graduate of a good junior college where his grades were all A's and B's. Tom interviews Jim and is even more favorably impressed. He tells the personnel manager that he would like to have Jim as his private secretary. He adds that the vacancy will not materialize for two months and suggests that something might be done to help Jim overcome his nervousness. If you were the personnel manager, what would you do? Follow the problem-solving method given in Chapter 9 in arriving at your decision.

Chapter 11

*Coping with
discrimination*

Recognizing Discrimination

Harold and James were hired at the same time. The high school janitor, Mr. Diamond, needed help and these two young men were employed to work part-time, before and after school. James was black. His family was the only nonwhite family in the school district of the small community. Soon it became obvious that Harold's work assignments were easier and more interesting than James'. James often got the dirty jobs. Harold was permitted to choose the hours he worked and he picked the hours after school. James was left with the early morning hours to work. Both made occasional mistakes; both worked hard. After several weeks, though, Mr. Diamond began to call attention to every mistake James made. Harold, it seemed, could do no wrong. Eventually, James was fired and another employee hired. James was a victim of unfair treatment—discrimination.

"That's not fair!" Have you ever found yourself in a situation where these words erupted in your mind—or from your lips? We all have a sense of fairness, and when it is violated, we feel very uncomfortable. *Discrimination* is a term that is used to describe unfair treatment of a particular person due to race, sex, age, religious affiliation, handicap, etc. *Prejudice* or "prejudgment" is an opinion that is formed without taking the time or trouble to judge in a fair manner. Prejudice allows us to treat

171

Illus. 11–1. Prejudice: People Suffer Emotionally and Materially

that person in a less-than-fair way. *Stereotypes* are pictures of people based on prejudices. Both prejudice and stereotypes lead to discrimination. People suffer emotionally as well as materially from discrimination. This chapter will take a look at discrimination and some of the options available to cope—or deal—with discrimination.

Discrimination, prejudice, and stereotyping are so much a part of our lives that we may hardly notice them. All too often our prejudices feel comfortable. We do not even think about them. We may even endure the discomforts of prejudice *against* us in order to keep a job. Today, however, there is an effort to make people conscious of their prejudices. Laws prohibit discriminatory practices on the basis of race, sex, religion, national origin, or physical or emotional handicaps.

In the case of Harold, James, and Mr. Diamond, all three persons involved were at fault. Mr. Diamond, even though he probably did not consider himself to be prejudiced, did not take the time to consider James as a person. He treated him unfairly. James was at fault for accepting the unfair treatment. He should have been aware of the discrimination and taken appropriate action to remedy it. Harold was also at fault for accepting the advantages he was receiving.

When prejudice becomes a part of your personality as a worker or when you learn to accept unfair treatment based on prejudice, a type of decay sets in. Work becomes less satisfying. Often, your productivity will decrease. In order to be a better worker, you must remove these barriers to productivity and job satisfaction. You need to learn to recognize and fight against discrimination in the workplace. You must be sensitive to what is going on around you and must recognize your personal prejudices in order to change them. This increased awareness is the first step in coping with discrimination in employment situations.

What the Law Provides

The Civil Rights Act became law in 1964. Title VII of that legislation was amended in 1972. According to this Act, employers are not allowed to discriminate in hiring, firing, layoffs, wages, promotions, or training. To make sure regulations are enforced, the Equal Employment Opportunity Commission (EEOC) was created. This agency receives and evaluates complaints, either trying to work out the problem or referring the complaint to the courts.

One of the positive results of the Civil Rights Act has been *affirmative action* which requires an employer to initiate efforts to correct any discriminatory employment practices. In recent years, due to the effect of these laws, job announcements have included phrases stating that the employer is nondiscriminatory with respect to race, creed, color, sex, age, national origin, or handicap.

Race, Color, and National Origin

During the process of recruiting and selecting workers, employers are required, by law, to do and to avoid certain topics. Interview questions concerning race, color, or ethnic background are prohibited. An employer may ask whether the applicant is a citizen of the United States. Questions regarding ability to read or speak foreign languages are also permitted, but questions regarding ancestry or native language are prohibited.

Religion

As a job applicant, you will be advised concerning normal hours or days of work required by the employer. An employer may ask if you are willing to work the required schedule. An employer may not, however, quiz you about your religious denomination, religious affiliations, or religious holidays.

Sex and Family Status

An employer may not ask your marital status. You do not need to indicate whether you are single, engaged, married, divorced, or separated. Questions regarding the number and ages of children or pregnancy are not allowed. An applicant may be asked if it will be possible to meet specific work schedules or if there are any activities, commitments, or responsibilities that may hinder the employee in meeting work attendance requirements. Other questions which may allow the employer to learn about your family status (without directly asking) can relate to expected duration on the job or anticipated absences. These

Illus. 11-2. Recognize discrimination in the workplace and fight it.

Photography by Owen Brown

Would you hire your daughter?

UN We Believe

questions may only be asked if they are asked of *all* applicants and are weighed equally in evaluations for both sexes.

Handicaps

Physical or mental handicaps may affect a person's ability to perform certain tasks. An employer, therefore, has a right to know about any handicap that may affect performance on a job. Inquiries may be made as to whether an applicant has a mental or physical handicap which should be considered in job placement. General questions that address handicaps or health conditions which do not directly relate to job performance are *not* allowed.

Age

While an employer may require a work permit (issued by school authorities) providing proof of age, an employer may not require a birth certificate as proof of age *before* hiring. Keep in mind that, in some situations, it is illegal to discriminate against an older *or* younger person during the hiring process.

Character

Traditionally there is discrimination and prejudice in the workplace against those whose character does not meet with the general standards of society. Criminals, members of subversive organizations, those who are poor credit risks, and others who are considered to be "undesirables" are often not allowed to work even though their abilities to perform in a given occupation are not impaired by the low esteem our society gives them. In many cases, however, the law requires that such individuals should have equal opportunity in employment with people of "acceptable" character.

An important regulation helps prevent discrimination against people who may have been arrested for, but not convicted of a crime. It prohibits inquiry as to whether a job applicant has ever been arrested. Questions concerning an applicant's *conviction* (if so, when, where, and disposition of the case) are allowed. No questions may be raised regarding your credit rating, charge accounts, or other financial matters. Finally, you may be asked about the type of education and experience you obtained in military service as it relates to a particular job, but you may not be asked what type of discharge you received.

As you consider the various laws and rules that apply to the prevention of discrimination in hiring, remember that the law alone cannot create fairness and equity. Agencies (such as the EEOC) have been especially set up to enforce these regulations. The other essential element (besides the law and the agencies) needed to combat discrimination is *you*. You must be aware of your rights as well as the rights of others. If you feel discrimination is being practiced, you must take the steps to alert the involved parties.

Sexual Harassment

Thus far, some highlights of your legal rights in employment have been discussed. This section is concerned with another type of discrimination—sexual harassment.

Sexual harassment in the workplace constitutes conduct by another employee which focuses on an individual's sexual role at the expense of that individual's role as a worker. Sexual harassment may consist of looks, remarks, or may go as far as physical assault. It can occur at any level of an organization. Supervisors may be harassed by subordinates as well as supervisors harassing subordinates.

The consequences of such abuse can lead to a good deal of personal sacrifice. A person may feel obligated to quit a job due to harassment or may even be fired from the job for resistance. The equal opportunity laws and civil rights agencies provide help for those who feel they are being sexually harassed.

If you feel you are being harassed on the job, remember that you have the *right* to be free from pressure or abuse. Some forms of harassment (such as physical assault) are crimes. Do not hesitate, in that case, to go to your local police department. If the harassment is not specifically a crime, there are other remedies. Unions and personnel departments can provide internal contacts. Keep in mind that you may file complaints on a federal level (with the EEOC) and on a local level (with human rights agencies). Finally, if you are being harassed, let the person know that this behavior is unacceptable. You have the right to resist!

Discrimination Among Co-Workers

Eighteen years ago Margaret had been very successful as a receptionist in a dentist's office. She had enjoyed the work and now wanted to return to the job market. She refreshed her professional skills by taking two adult education classes. She prepared a personal data sheet, updated her references from former employers, and began the interviewing process. But things seemed different now. It seemed that people were talking down to her—treating her with less respect. When she finally obtained a position, it was as a file clerk, where she had little contact with the public. During the first week on the job, Margaret began to pick up a clear message: people were treating her as if she were slow. Her co-workers seemed less friendly than she had expected. What was Margaret's problem? Was Margaret a victim of age discrimination?

The Constitution of the United States offers many kinds of protection from prejudice and discrimination. Many state and local regulations also contribute to the enactment of the rights we have. But basic human nature—the attitudes of those with whom you associate—cannot be entirely controlled by legislation and law enforcement. Keep this in mind when you deal with discrimination.

Avoiding, Fighting, or Resisting Discrimination

To this point we have considered the many different aspects of discrimination and prejudice in the world of work. You have been encouraged to be alert and sensitive to discrimination and prejudice. Our concern now turns to actually dealing with discrimination. There are several options available to you if you feel you are a victim of discrimination. In this section, we will discuss four of these alternatives.

Turn and Walk Away

There may be situations where you consider the costs of confrontation too high when dealing with discrimination. You may feel that the least painful choice is to walk away from the pressure. You might resign your position or ask for a transfer to free yourself from a situation. You may even refuse a job offer feeling that the pressure of prejudice from your subordinates or co-workers will be too great.

Simply turning and walking away *seems* like the least painful option, but it leaves you with little hope or satisfaction. In the long run, it can affect others who may be in your position. Prejudices will not be brought to light. Unfair practices will continue. And by leaving, you will be helping to maintain that prejudice. Keep your own rights in mind. Then, turning and walking away may not seem so painless.

Revenge

If you are a victim of discrimination, your first impulse may be to "get even" with the offender. This alternative usually does more harm than good. Often it simply increases the prejudice and, as a result, the discrimination. Revenge can take many forms—from vandalizing to physical assault. Be aware that these

Illus. 11–3. Remember that human nature cannot be entirely controlled by legislation when dealing with discrimination.

Gerald L. French Photography / The PhotoFile

forms are against the law. Charges may be brought against you. You could find yourself without a job *and* with a court record. If your strategy for dealing with discrimination includes revenge, carefully consider the consequences. They are far more damaging than any pleasure you may receive from "getting even." Recognize the folly of revenge.

Positive Resistance with Patience

Occasionally you can overcome prejudice with time and patience. The very nature of prejudice—based on stereotypes of the individual *or* the group—is not only unfair, but most often is not an accurate picture. Demonstrating that you do not fit the image, by doing your best job, can do much to reduce or eliminate the prejudice. For instance, when Margaret reorganized the entire filing system (eliminating the problem of misindexed files), her co-workers began to seek her advice. They no longer recognized the difference in age. They no longer avoided contact with her.

Positive resistance does not mean that you should ignore or endure the prejudice. Positive resistance implies clearly recognizing *and* confronting the prejudice. It means letting your co-workers know that you are aware of the prejudice, uncomfortable with it, but determined to prove them wrong.

Unfortunately, not all discrimination can be eliminated with positive resistance. The last section deals with the strongest means of dealing with discrimination.

Come Right Out and Fight

This chapter has discussed your basic human rights. These rights are protected by laws and regulations of our government. If you feel your rights are being violated, you have remedies under the law for dealing with this discrimination.

Your first action should be to attempt to correct the situation from an on-the-job perspective. Contact a member of your personnel department or union. An investigation will be conducted. If just cause is found, grievance procedures can be initiated. This may be as far as you need to go to correct the discrimination. If you receive no satisfaction from these sources, your next step will be to either contact an attorney or a governmental agency dealing with discrimination. On a local level, you may contact any human rights agency. On the federal level, you should contact the Equal Employment Opportunity Commission (EEOC). Be aware that if you have a legal case against your employer for discrimination, you must be prepared to face a not-always-sympathetic public, often including your co-workers. If you decide to proceed with court remedies, don't make it a halfhearted attempt. Backing away after you have taken the initiative can be worse than losing. Always keep in mind your right to be judged for yourself—free of stereotypes and prejudices. You have the right to fight discrimination.

Questions and Projects

1. Have you ever been stereotyped? Have your family or friends had this happen to them? Describe five ways that you or your close relatives or friends might experience prejudice from an employer or co-worker based on stereotypes.

2. This chapter highlights the importance of being aware of discrimination. Analyze your work situation.

  a. Prepare a list of the ways that you are, or that you suspect you might be, subject to discrimination. Consider both favorable and unfavorable possibilities.
  b. Prepare a list of ways that you might be showing preference or discrimination (favorable as well as unfavorable).
  c. Share and discuss the results of your analysis with others in your class.

3. Interview or invite as a guest speaker someone in your community who may have been involved in problems with discrimination and prejudice in the world of work.

4. Ask a librarian to help you, if necessary, to search out documented cases of discrimination in the workplace. Newspapers, records of court cases, and periodicals are possible sources. Study one case and write a report on it. Present your report in class.

5. Interview or invite as a guest speaker a personnel director of a large company in your community. Ask the personnel director about problems the company may have with discrimination and what is being done to remedy those problems. Write or give a report on what you learn.

6. During an employment interview, you should be able to ask questions that would help you determine whether or not discrimination is present. For each of the following possibilities, write a question that might provide clues to:

  a. Racial prejudice.
  b. Prejudice toward a handicap.
  c. Prejudice toward young workers; toward older workers.
  d. Prejudice toward women or men in hiring.
  e. Prejudice toward someone with a prison record.
  f. Favoritism toward people of a particular race.

Case Problems

1. Racial Discrimination.

Reread the story of Harold and James at the beginning of this chapter.

1. Put yourself in James' position. What action could you have taken to prevent or correct this situation?
2. Put yourself in Harold's position. What are your responsibilities as a friend and co-worker to James? What are your responsibilities to Mr. Diamond? What steps might you take to help correct the situation?

2. Age Discrimination.

After receiving an outstanding application for the position of teller at Security First Bank, the personnel director decided to call Charles Nelson in for an interview. Charles walked into the managerial offices of the bank the morning of the interview. The personnel director entered the outer office and saw Charles. He said, "Sir, these are the managerial offices. The tellers are located in the front section of the bank." Charles replied, "I'm here for an interview with the personnel director." The director looked at the floor for a minute and then said, "Quite truthfully, I had no idea . . . Your age . . ." What could Charles Nelson do?

3. Modeling?

Alice had graduated from a two-year fashion merchandising program and obtained a good position as an executive trainee for a large department store. Her main job was as salesperson in the camera department. The store advertising manager, George Smith, asked Alice to model in some of the store's newspaper ads. During one of the picture-taking sessions, George Smith appeared and stayed for the entire session. After the session, he walked over to Alice and said, "I'm working on a swimsuit promotion and doing the photography myself. It's not really for the store. How would you like to pick up a few extra dollars by working overtime on this project." There was a pause.

1. Are there any clues in this case to indicate something about George Smith's motives?
2. What are the important questions that Alice must answer as she considers how to respond to George Smith?

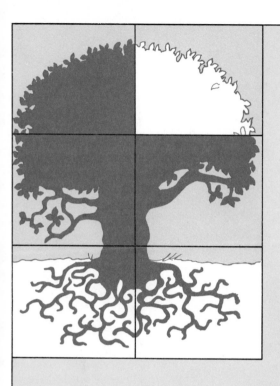

PART FIVE
Communicating

Chapter 12

Opening communication channels

Suppose you are trapped in a giant bubble. No one can hear you; you can hear no one else. Then another bubble comes into your vision. Someone else is trapped in a bubble just like yours. Can you talk to that other person? Can you become friends? No, not as long as the bubbles remain intact. If you have trouble talking to other people, if you get stage fright when you have to talk before a group, if it is hard for you to say what you feel, you are trapped in just such a psychological bubble. How can you escape? How can you establish contact and communicate?

Studies have shown that babies who are not communicated with by being held, talked to, and loved, frequently die within a year. You may have a relationship with someone in which you are having trouble getting through to that person. That relationship can die if you let things go on the way they are. Communication is, literally, a lifeline. To be successful in employment you *must* "plug in" to the communication network.

Overcome Barriers to Communication

Even when you are communicating fairly well, you may still be enclosed in a bubble of sorts. Good communication has another ingredient. What you say and write must mean the same

Illus. 12–1. Barriers to Communication: Make an Effort to Overcome Them

to your listener or reader as it does to you—and that isn't easy. You must get *through* your bubble by speaking and writing in ways that will make the bubble break up. When you do that, the other person's bubble will break up, too. Others will be able to understand what you are trying to say or write.

Poor Choice of Words

The first barrier can be overcome by choosing your words carefully. You must use words that will not be misunderstood. Secondly, those words must have the same feeling tone to the other person as they do to you. With some words there is no difficulty. A word like *slimy*, for example, has the same feeling tone to most of us. But other words, such as *establishment*, and *liberal*, may be considered either good words or bad words, depending on a person's background and experiences.

It would be so simple if all emotionally charged words were reacted to by everyone in the same way. You could then deliberately avoid using "dangerous" words; but such a simple solution is out of our reach. You say what you say because you are the kind of person you are. In other words, you speak through your bubble—some authors call it your *filter*. Furthermore, you hear what the other person says through that same filter. Someone else, with a different makeup and different experiences (and thus a different filter) will pick out different meanings from those same words. If you are suspicious by nature, you think other people are suspicious, too. You read into any statement made to you some part of your own characteristics.

Prejudice

Another barrier to good communication is that most of us want to skip the unpleasant things in life, particularly if they are a threat to the way we like to think of ourselves, our beliefs, and our prejudices. Each of us has had the experience of trying to persuade friends to abandon foolish ideas in favor of our sensible ones. The friends resort to a simple and effective countermeasure; they do not hear our arguments. We all have equal access to this device, by the way. We read what we want to read, we hear what we want to hear.

Acceptance

The hardest lesson to be learned as you attempt to open communication channels with other people is that change can come only through the wishes of the person involved. You may see others acting foolishly, making mistakes, or taking the wrong turn. You may have made some of the same mistakes yourself, and your natural tendency is to point out the error of their ways. You will learn, however, that you cannot change others through pointing out their faults. In fact, such a step usually makes matters worse. Change comes because the person wants to change—and through no other way. The principle involved in changing someone is *acceptance*—acceptance of yourself and acceptance of others.

Accept yourself. What does "Accept yourself" mean? Simply this: Work every day—for just a few minutes at a time—to accept yourself the way you are. Don't dwell on your faults; just accept them. Say to yourself, "Yes, I know you put things off until the last minute. I know you are sarcastic whenever you are afraid someone is going to hurt you. I know you are afraid to take the first step in getting acquainted with another person. But I like you anyway." Do you know what happens when you accept yourself the way you are? With acceptance comes the ability to change. As long as you defend yourself, make excuses, blame your troubles on others, you will be unable to change. You will have a sort of mental paralysis that literally keeps you from getting rid of any of the qualities within you that are hurting your chances for success and happiness.

When you take that one hard step of acceptance, however, you seem to release a brake inside of you. No longer will you be driving yourself with your brakes on. You will be free from the drag of that nonacceptance brake. With that brake released, you will find it easier to change. Don't forget, though, that accepting yourself is not easy. It is, in fact, terribly hard. Don't try to build self-acceptance too quickly. Just work at it for a few minutes at a time. One psychologist has mentioned five minutes as the goal you should set. For five minutes at a time, look at yourself squarely. Say, "Yes, that's the way I am. But I'm still OK."

Accept others. The second step in acceptance seems to follow the first one naturally. After you have learned to accept yourself, you can begin to accept others. When you have learned to look squarely at your own faults, without criticism, you can look at the shortcomings of others without trying to change them. The "brake release" effect seems to work with others just as well as it does with you. When you can look at your bullying customer and say, "This customer is angry with me, but it may be caused by something else. This customer is a good person underneath," you will release your customer's brake. Laura Huxley has written a book called *You Are Not the Target.* This book says that most of the cruel things said to others are not really directed at them. The "picked on" person may have just been around when the speaker defended himself or herself by lashing out at the closest person. When *you do not defend yourself,* but merely accept others for what they are, your attitude will tell others that you are still their friend. When they feel your accepting attitude, in spite of what they have said or done, they will be able to release the brake that is holding them back. They will be able to change.

Improve Your Awareness

Awareness is a quality that is especially important when you work in groups. It means that you are aware of the feelings and personalities of the people who work with you. You know which areas can be discussed with your co-workers and which should be left alone. You know when others would rather not be talked with and when they would welcome an invitation to lunch. If you are aware of others, you will spend more of your time looking outside yourself instead of looking inward. Awareness grows as you become less self-centered.

Awareness has another side, as well. Be aware of the flow of authority in the firm in which you work. This means that you will "go through channels." You will take your questions and problems to your immediate supervisor. That person carries them to the next level of management, and so on. If you should go over the head of your immediate supervisor, you fail to show respect for this position. You should study the organization chart of the firm, which lists the officers of the company, the heads of departments, supervisors, and so on. You will then know how the whole organization works; you will also have a clearer picture of your position. This will show you the path downward and upward for directions, information, suggestions, and grievances. It will also show you where your work ultimately goes, a knowledge that adds to your feeling of worth.

Empathy

It isn't what you say, it's the *way* you say it that sometimes makes the difference. If you are to improve *tone*, or the way you say it, you must develop the traits of *empathy* and tact. (Empathy means to see and feel something just the way another person sees and feels. In a sense, you feel *with* the other person.) You may think there is no place in the business world for empathy, but this is not true. What you will probably find is too little time for the expression of empathy. In any case, you should be concerned with being empathetic yourself, not with having others empathize with you. Your employer is usually working under a much greater strain than you are. You should be empathetic to those problems and understanding of any impatience and irritability.

You will have many opportunities to show understanding and empathy. If you are sensitive to the feelings of others, you will try to make them feel at ease. This ability to make others feel at ease is an important factor in getting along with others. It also helps them to feel at ease about sharing their real inner feelings with you. If you are relaxed and natural yourself, it is because you are able to think of others instead of yourself.

In addition to putting others at ease, be careful to treat others as you would like to be treated. Speak in a friendly manner to new employees; take the time to be kind to those who are in trouble; be sensitive to moods and do not intrude on another's desire for privacy.

The Art of Persuasion

The art of persuasion is basically the art of breaking down the barriers to communication—gently or forcibly—so that your message can get through. You have been using techniques of persuasion in your work and play all through your life. You have learned that some techniques are effective and some are not. At the age of three or four, you may have tried the technique of lying on the floor and screaming to get your own way. You may have discovered, too, that this didn't work too well at age nine or ten. In this same way, you may have tried and discarded many techniques of persuasion. You should sharpen up some techniques you now use and perhaps become familiar with some entirely new ones.

Develop A Friendly Attitude

> One dark and gloomy afternoon, a woman, modestly dressed, came into a furniture store. One of the older salespeople said, "Don't spend any time with her. She'll look and look and never buy anything." But one of the younger salespeople stepped forward with a friendly greeting and showed the woman furniture for the rest of the afternoon. Then, as the older salesperson had predicted, she left without buying anything. A few weeks later, however, the younger salesperson was pleased and surprised when asked to help decorate the new mansion of the Andrew Carnegies. The woman whom the salesperson had helped so patiently was Louise Carnegie.

A friendly personality is an asset anywhere. If your work brings you into contact with many people, a friendly attitude is essential. If you were born with a liking for people, you should do well. But if strangers make you hide in your shell, don't give up. The technique of being courteous is a good way to begin working on creating a friendly personality. At first, though, you may have to work at it. Take every opportunity to say "thank you" with a smile. Try to follow the rules of good etiquette and, after a while, you will actually *feel* more friendly.

Study Psychology

Why do people behave as they do? In other words, why do people act like people? Most people who have watched television shows and have read popular articles can tell you all about inferiority complexes, overcompensation, and so on. Most psychologists, however, believe they are still learning about people. They dislike giving the impression that human nature is an open book. Still, research continues at an ever-increasing rate, and more and more of the complexities of people are being understood. We do know some of the factors causing behavior. Some of them are conditioning, or building up habitual responses to certain words, rules, and other stimuli. Some examples of these are illnesses (particularly those affecting the nervous system), conflicts (both conscious and unconscious), and the pressures exerted by the different groups that are active in a person's life.

Such knowledge of psychology is helpful in understanding ourselves and others. A beginner in business makes a wise choice when enrolling in courses in psychology. Although a discussion of general psychology is beyond the scope of this book, some psychological principles and techniques that are particularly useful in business will be mentioned.

"Yes" Works Better Than "No"

If you want to persuade someone to do something, you will be more successful if the discussion is positive or pleasant. If others like you as a person, they will be more willing to listen to what you have to say. The best way to keep your dealings with others as pleasant as you can is to look for "yes" situations and to watch out for the things that have unpleasant consequences.

Help the Other Person Feel Important

You will not succeed if you build yourself up at the expense of other people. If you boast about how well you are doing, you will make others feel doubtful about their own success. If you treat others as if you were on a higher plane, you will again make them doubt their own value. For example, if you begin by saying, "You may not understand this, but . . ." you will make your listener feel smaller. Another statement that causes your listener to feel small is to say, "It ought to be perfectly clear that . . ." The way to make others feel tall and important is to ask for their advice, to get their point of view, to make them a part of any decision you make. Look for opportunities to give recognition, to build others up, to make them feel ten feet tall.

An important technique in helping others to feel important is learning how to play second fiddle. This may seem odd, yet it is effective. If you watch successful salespeople, for example, you will notice their easy, relaxed manner. This manner sets the stage; it provides the kind of atmosphere needed in selling. If this atmosphere is friendly, if the customer feels important, and if the salesperson can explain the product and answer questions intelligently and courteously, the customer will feel free to choose but will be much more likely to choose in favor of the salesperson.

Ignore The Negative

When others complain about your actions or job performance, let them talk. Just listen attentively. As you listen, ignore the part of the conversation that sounds as if it is directed at

Illus. 12–2. Ignore negative statements that sound directed at you personally.

you personally. Negative statements of this kind are best forgotten. Just concentrate on what you can learn and give the complainer the opportunity to speak.

Reward The Positive

When someone says something positive about you or your company, respond warmly. Such a response is rewarding to the other person, and you have learned from previous chapters that rewarded responses are more likely to be repeated than those that are not rewarded. Most of us have trouble, however, in accepting compliments. Practice saying something warm, something "giving" back to the person who compliments you. Instead of saying, "Oh, it was nothing," show the other person how the compliment made you feel. If you say, "It makes me feel good to hear you say that," you are giving the other person warmth in return for those kind words to you. Accepting compliments warmly takes practice, and it is never too late to begin.

Listening to Communicate

Of the three ways of sending and receiving communication—writing, speaking, and listening—the most difficult is listening. Yet good listening is a useful art and one that can be practiced every day. If you want to improve your listening ability, you should (1) concentrate on the speaker, (2) take well-organized notes, and (3) avoid the stumbling blocks of good listening.

Concentrate on the Speaker

In face-to-face listening you may find yourself planning your reply instead of concentrating on what the speaker is saying. This same tendency may be your downfall when you listen to a lecture. Instead of concentrating on the speaker, you may find your mind wandering to personal matters where, indeed, you plan what you are going to say. To avoid such distracting thoughts, listen for hints as to the speaker's organization plan. Listen to the title (or it may be listed in the program). Write

Illus. 12–3. Concentrate to improve your listening skills.

Courtesy of Government Development Bank for Puerto Rico

down the title. Now certain main divisions may seem logical to you. Write these divisions down, numbering them with Roman numerals about a half page apart.

Take Notes in Outline Form

One of the common fallacies of note-taking is that you feel you must take down nearly everything the speaker says. A better plan is to listen a lot and write a little. Remember: Listening is the receiving part of communication. Understanding is the key. Understand the main points of what the speaker is saying. If you spend all your time getting down words, you will be sure to miss some of these main points. Under your main divisions, then (numbered with Roman numerals), you will write subdivisions (A, B, and C). Leave plenty of space between these subdivisions. You can then put the speaker's afterthoughts in their logical place.

Avoid the Stumbling Blocks of Good Listening

You must be mentally alert if you are to get the most out of your listening practice. To "stay on the beam" with the speaker, you must avoid the stumbling blocks of daydreaming and paying attention to distractions.

Daydreaming. The enemy of daydreaming is activity. When you feel your attention wandering, begin to write industriously. Look at the speaker; anticipate what will be said next; think of possible examples that might be used to underline the points made.

Attending to distractions. Your surroundings may distract your attention; noise in the corridor, street noises, latecomers, whispering in the audience. Moreover, the speaker may distract you by appearance, pronunciation, or voice. To all these distractions, you must turn a deaf ear. Concentrate on the content of the talk. Let all unimportant matters go. Remember, too, that listening is work. Be sure to work at it when you listen.

Creative Listening

In face-to-face communication, listening is especially important. In fact, listening now becomes a creative process. To develop the skill of creative listening, just follow these steps: First of all, you should watch the person who is talking; there is much to be learned from an expression. If you mentally put yourself in the place of the speaker, you will gain even more because you will know how the speaker feels.

The second part of creative listening is to organize in your mind what the speaker is saying. If you are being told something that you are to do, it is better if you can take notes. If this is impossible at the moment, however, you can gain considerably from mentally putting the important statements made by the speaker in logical order.

The third factor is interest. You should show that you are interested in what is being told you. An alert expression will follow suit if you *are* alert. This expression will tell your speaker more than words could tell. If you are interested, however, you will also want to say something to further the statements that are being made. Such responses as, "I see," "That's a good sugges-tion," and "I'll get right at it," will help the speaker and also help you. In all aspects of conversation, whether of speaking or listening, success depends on cooperation.

Questions and Projects

1. One of the most difficult ways of becoming more outgoing is taking the initiative in meeting new people. To help you overcome this universal tendency toward "inwardness," you are to meet, entirely through your own efforts, 10 people (of any age). Exactly four weeks from today you are to report the results of the project on a separate sheet of paper in the following form:

1. Name	Short Biography	Situation (How we met)	Opener (What I said)

Remember, you must have ten names and *you* must make the first move. No one else may introduce you. The short biography should contain at least four items of information about each person.

Follow your report with a paragraph of evaluation of the experi-ence. How did it affect you? Will it change your future behavior? What have you learned about people in general?

2. Practice the following suggestions for remembering names. Report whether the suggestions were effective for you.

  a. When a person is being introduced, be sure that you not only hear the name but know how it is spelled. If there is doubt in your mind about the spelling, ask the individual to spell it; never ask the person who introduced you.
  b. When you have the name, turn your attention to the face. Look at the person and in some way associate the name with the face.
  c. File this association away in your memory, *knowing* that you will remember that person next time you meet.
  d. Whenever you meet a person, make it a point to address that person by name at the beginning of your conversation.

3. One of the hurdles you must conquer in getting a job is talking with an interviewer. How do you rate when you talk with strangers? If you feel insecure in this respect, do some practicing. Talk with someone whom you do not know about employment matters. Possible sources are librarians, teachers in your school whom you do not know, the placement director in your school. Try to get over your fear before you go to an actual interview.

4. You have a friend who is extremely interested in current politics. In order to carry on an intelligent conversation, go over one of the newsmagazines for this week. Choose five topics that might interest your friend and learn something about each topic.

5. The next time you are talking with a friend, try this experiment: See if you can remain silent exactly half the time. You may need to spur your friend with such remarks as, "And then what happened?" See if you are talking too much or too little as a general rule.

6. Which of the following descriptions would you use to describe the way you meet people during an interview? What can you do to improve your rating?

Lacks ease	Slightly nervous	Averted eyes
Nervous	At ease	Great poise

7. Make a list of ten words you use occasionally that have an unpleasant emotional connotation or coloring. Next, see if you can find a synonym for each of the ten words, each synonym to have a pleasant connotation. Try to make the pleasant words a part of your vocabulary, at the same time eliminating the unpleasant words.

8. Practice the suggestions given in the "Listening to Communicate" section in this chapter in one of your lecture classes. Do you think that this method of taking notes has helped you? Discuss.

9. Begin a conversation with someone whose remarks usually irritate you. Let the other person talk; you listen. Do not interrupt for at least three minutes. See if you can detect *why* this person holds these beliefs, if there is some logical basis for this point of view. Now, answer with a compromising statement, such as, "You do have a point there, but what do you think about. . . ?" Ask an intelligent question, one that shows you were really listening. Did this activity improve your relationship with this particular person? Discuss.

Case Problems

1. Yeah!

Lena Washington, a recent high school graduate, thoroughly enjoys her first job as a salesperson in the Foss Drugstore. She is efficient and keeps herself busy tidying up the shelves when business lags. Nevertheless, the store manager, Mr. Valdes, is sharp with Lena, especially when she talks to him. He is friendly and sociable to Nathan Knight, the other salesperson; and this fact is disturbing to Lena. Lena likes Nathan but finds she must often help him out of careless mistakes. One day Mr. Valdes listens in on Lena's conversation over the telephone with a customer.

> Customer: "Do you carry Acme travel clocks?"
> Lena: "Yeah, we have it."
> Customer: "Do you have it in blue?"
> Lena: "No, just green."
> Customer: "What is the price?"
> Lena: "Ten bucks."
> Customer: "Thank you. I'll try another store."
> Lena: "Sorry."

Later, Lena approaches Nathan in tears, explaining that Mr. Valdes called her to his office and curtly told her to let Nathan answer the phone from now on. Nathan answers that Mr. Valdes probably objects to Lena's way of speaking.

1. Assuming you are Lena, solve this problem using the five-step method explained in Chapter 9.
2. Why is it Lena's problem, rather than that of Mr. Valdes?

2. Word Lack or Judgment Lack?

Alex Curtis took dictation from Joan Grayson, the head of the advertising department. Joan was a rapid speaker and occasionally slurred words to the point that Alex could not understand them. One day during dictation, Joan used the word *hybrid*, but Alex heard the word as *high-bred*. Not getting the idea, Alex interrupted, "Ms. Grayson, do you mean high-bred?" Joan was annoyed at losing her train of thought. "Use better judgment," she said, "and don't interrupt."

1. Assuming that Alex had been working at this postion for more than six months, is there some way he could have avoided this situation?
2. How should Alex have reacted to this reprimand?
3. What clues should he have had from the context to help him in deciding which word was intended?

4. Is there a grammatical rule that might have helped him in this case?
5. Some dictators prefer to be interrupted during dictation. What personality clues would help you in deciding when to ask and when not to ask a question during dictation?

3. The Seamy Side.

Louise Ryan is a secretary for a small-town newspaper publisher. One part of her job is to keep subscribers and advertisers satisfied as far as possible and to try to create a feeling of goodwill between the publisher and the community. One day, when she answers the telephone, a voice demands to talk to the managing editor. Louise replies that the managing editor is not in the office and asks if she can help. The person answers in a loud voice, using abusive language. Louise puts the receiver down with a bang. The telephone rings for some time, but she refuses to listen again to such talk.

1. What is the correct attitude toward difficult individuals in situations such as this one?
2. Was Louise behaving in an objective manner?
3. Why do you think Louise acted as she did?
4. What might have Louise done that would have served the publisher in a better way?

4. A Place for Sensitivity.

Ann Madison is responsible for admitting patients in a large medical clinic. Her task is to fill out routine records concerning patients for the files. The data are of a factual nature and contain no medical information. When talking with a middle-aged man, she observes that he is embarrassed by having to supply such information as his name, age, address, and business. When she has recorded these answers, Ann says to the patient, "And now will you tell me why you have come here?"

"Look, lady," he answers, "is it the practice for a patient to have to give you that kind of information?"

Ann answers, "I'm sorry, sir. I'm only doing my job. My instructions from Dr. Reynolds are that I must get this information."

1. Do you feel that Ann was sensitive to the needs of others?
2. About what types of needs or feelings are some people very sensitive?
3. Should Ann have insisted that the man answer her question? How would you have handled this situation? Why?

Chapter 13

Getting your message across

Connie and Pat were enjoying their coffee break when Elsie walked in, said "Hi" as she obtained a drink from the vending machine, and left. "What's with Elsie?" said Pat. "She hasn't said two words in pleasant conversation during the month she has been working here." Connie answered, "Either she is a snob or she's just plain shy—I can't decide which." "Oh, I'm sure she's not a snob," said Pat, "I get the impression that she wants to be one of the group. She just has a hard time carrying on a conversation. And she seems to avoid talking with any of the supervisors whenever possible." "Well, if that's the case, maybe we should try to help her," Connie replied. "But what should we tell her?"

What is your greatest social fear? Wearing the wrong clothes? Probably not. Most people are much less concerned over fashion than they were in the past. Table etiquette? No. The casual mode of entertaining has almost eliminated worry about which fork to use. The one fear nearly everyone has is that of carrying on a conversation with someone who is not a close friend or member of the family. The difficulty arises when we must talk with those we know slightly, or perhaps not at all. You may be fearful, ill at ease, afraid you will be judged by what you say.

How can we overcome fear of conversation? Actually, the secret of success in oral communication is one that has been

Illus. 13–1. Giving Information: Be Yourself to Communicate Most Effectively

mentioned before—just being yourself. Part of the strain that causes feelings of uneasiness stems from trying to impress others with a false personality. But if we pretend to be what we are not, we must be constantly on guard. This guardedness may be thought by others to be an attack against some weakness of their own. They, then, will defend themselves with similar pretenses. This vicious circle can produce nothing but disaster.

Don't Just Stand There—Say Something!

You have already learned that the human element is the most important one in business. If you can get along successfully with others, you will have many of the qualities you need for success. Most of getting along with others involves conversation. You must ask others to do things for you; you must express appreciation for a kindness; you must persuade a sales prospect; you must put your customer or caller at ease. All of this involves conversation. The importance of the ability to establish friendly relations with others cannot be overemphasized. Much of your success and happiness will depend on it. Some of the specific areas in your business life where conversational skill will help you are discussed in this chapter.

Improving Personal Relations

You will improve your relations with others if you improve your conversational skills. The secret lies in making your listener feel important. If you just talk about yourself and your own accomplishments, you probably will be considered a bore. If you talk sincerely about the accomplishments of your listener, you will have a fascinated audience. All people are interested in themselves; few feel properly appreciated. For example, the story is told of a man who picked ten names at random from the telephone directory and sent them telegrams with a one-word message, "Congratulations." He signed his name and address to the wire and awaited results. Nine of the ten individuals wrote him warm letters of thanks. All of them stated they had not been aware that anyone knew of their recent accomplishments. Only one person wrote to ask, "Congratulations for what?"

Getting and Giving Information

Another way conversational skill can aid you is in giving and getting information. The teacher, the business owner, the supervisor—all must have the ability to talk conversationally to those whom they wish to instruct. Getting information is involved here, too; it is a two-way process. If you can ask sensible questions, if you can show with a nod or a smile that you understand, you will be using your conversational gifts to advantage.

Knowledge can be pursued in several ways. Some get their knowledge from books, some go on to higher levels of education; but one of the most effective ways to learn is by listening to those who know. Intelligent conversation can bring you the twin rewards of interest and information.

Getting Things Done

Conversation is also an aid to getting work done. If you can write conversationally, you will be able to persuade through letters. If you can lecture conversationally, large groups will give you closer attention. If you can talk to your staff conversationally, they will be more likely to follow your directions. A good conversationalist has a friendly interest in others. This interest is contagious. If you can express it, you will be more likely to receive it in return.

Ten Easy Lessons in Conversation

It is all very well to say you should be able to converse with others with ease. But such a statement is certain to bring the question "How?" The following paragraphs will tell you how; after that, you just need practice.

You Must Like People

If you don't like people in general, this will be your first task. It is helpful if you realize that *everyone* is insecure to some degree. So if you feel insecure about liking others, you are not the only one who feels as you do. One of the best ways of starting on your "people-liking" campaign is to act as if you did. You will be surprised at the reaction of others. You may even begin to like them!

Don't Talk Too Fast

Good conversation should be relaxing, so don't talk too fast. Otherwise you will find your feeling of tenseness spreading to your listeners. A good way to slow your speaking tempo down is by frequent pauses. Don't be afraid of silence. Constant chatter can be extremely wearing, and an occasional pause will point up what is said afterward. Clear enunciation is important. If you speak with a relaxed manner and with clear enunciation, you will find others listening to you. Your words will take on a new importance from your method of delivery.

Learn To Listen

One of the hardest lessons to learn is that of listening, but it is one of the most important. Specific suggestions about how to do this are found in the previous chapter. If you will think of your conversational group as a basketball team, for example, it may help you see the necessity of giving each player a chance at the basket. Throw the conversational ball to others; listen with concentration; show your interest in your face. Learning this one lesson well can make others think you are a gifted conversationalist. You won't need to say much yourself if you can make the conversation of others seem more important. A good listener must keep out all feelings of criticism, too. If you think to yourself, "This person is really dumb," you may show it in your manner, defeating all you have been trying to accomplish.

Avoid Total Disagreement

If you want to become extremely unpopular, just speak out for the viewpoint opposite to the one being expressed. When you contradict the speaker, you are guilty of being rude. Even more unpleasant, however, you will usually stop the conversation dead. A mild response is much more effective, even if the speaker has made a foolish remark. "Do you really think so?" may sound spineless to you in such circumstances, but it is better conversational tactics than a total contradiction, such as, "You are completely wrong!" Try to eliminate all feelings of competitiveness in conversation. There is no winner or loser; there should be, instead, a feeling of friendliness in a group talking together.

Don't Be Backward

If you are excessively shy, you may worry about yourself. Yet you may never have considered the effect of your shyness on others, for the backward conversationalist makes the others feel too forward. By fading into the background, you create an unnatural atmosphere that makes normal talkativeness seem excessive. Another difficulty with being overly shy is the tendency to appear cold and unfeeling to others. This makes people uncomfortable in your presence. Can you see how shyness, based on feelings of inferiority, will impress others as being based on self-centeredness? It is much better for you, and for the group in which you find yourself, to make an effort to be interested in others. If you start by showing interest in what others say, it won't be long before you will be able to say something, too.

Don't Hold Center Stage Too Long

If you tell a story, make it short. If you explain the way you think about something, hit the highlights only, leaving out the details. You must do this in order to leave space for others to talk, too. If you monopolize the conversation more than a moment or two, you will seem to be seeking the spotlight. This should be avoided, especially by the beginner in the art of conversation.

Watch Your Eye Contact

A very important part of talking in a group is looking at all of the members of the group. This makes them feel included; again, it builds up the other person. If you look at just one person as you speak, the others will feel excluded. It is hard to tear your eyes away from someone who seems to be responding to you; but if you are to converse well, you must make an effort to do so. Try looking first to your left, then to your right, and then straight ahead. As you look in each direction, focus your eyes on some feature of one of the persons in that area. It *is* hard to look listeners directly in the eye; but make yourself do it. It's very important.

Keep Your Statements Pleasant

When you first start developing your skill in conversation, you should avoid unpleasant topics, criticism of others, sarcasm, and pessimism. In fact, it would be a good idea to avoid them entirely. It is especially important, however, for the beginner to refrain from derogatory remarks. In the first place, few people admire the person who makes such remarks. In the second place, they destroy the spirit of friendship that is built up by good conversation.

Make Yourself Talk

The conversational beginner may have some trouble getting started. It is a good idea, therefore, to have some plan ready before you begin. You may decide to compliment one of the speakers; this is always a good approach. Just saying, "How interesting. I had never thought of that," is really praise of the other person's remarks. Or you can say, "Do you really think this will happen?" This is complimentary to the person speaking because it shows you are thinking about what has been said. Another opener for the beginner is a question. The speaker is always glad to have a question because this gives the chance to talk to a definite point. If someone has been talking about a hobby, for example, you might ask, "How long did it take you to learn the technique?" A question is another sincere form of flattery. It is an easy way, too, to get a conversation started.

Avoid Laying Down the Law

A good conversationalist keeps a tolerant attitude. If you preach, if you hand down judgments, others will not enjoy listening to you. The secret is to keep an open mind. A conversation should be a free exchange of ideas. No one person should try to dominate it. Avoid, then, giving the final word on any subject. This will permit other persons in the group to add what they think. This is one way of keeping the conversational ball rolling.

What to Say When

Many of us have no difficulty carrying on a conversation after it has been started, but we do have some trouble starting it. Is there any rule to help get that first minute of conversation under way? Think for a moment of the most common subject of casual conversation, the weather. Why do strangers who must say something to each other resort to, "Is it hot enough for you?" It's a safe topic, that's why. The other person is certain to have something to say on the subject. When starting a conversation, then, it is best to begin with something about which everyone has an opinion.

When you use a question as a conversation starter, be careful to choose one that cannot be answered by a flat *yes* or *no*. Instead of the question asked in the previous paragraph, which would be almost sure to be answered, "Yes," you might say, "How long has it been since we had a good rainstorm?" This isn't any more sparkling than the previous question, but it does require some thought and a more or less complete sentence in reply. Asking a question that requires a statement in answer will keep the conversation going for a time, at least.

Some questions should be avoided. These include personal questions, particularly those involving health and money. If you are in doubt as to whether a question is too personal, put yourself in the other person's shoes. Would you like someone to ask you why your nose is red and your eyes all puffy? Would you like someone to ask how much you paid for the clothes you are wearing, or how much your car cost? It is also wise, when starting a conversation, to avoid emotionally tinged subjects, such as religion and politics.

Talking With Your Supervisors

Beginning workers are frequently ill at ease when talking with their supervisors. A good tip to remember is a single word: *follow*. In most cases, it is better to let the other person lead the conversation and listen more than you talk. If your supervisor is thinking or is deeply engrossed with something, it's best to avoid conversation except for important matters. On the other hand, if your supervisor is in a humorous mood, follow the lead—laugh at the jokes. Tell one yourself! If you are asked

Illus. 13–2. Let your supervisor lead the conversation and listen carefully.

© *Carole Graham*

for your opinion on something, give it promptly, tactfully, and confidently. If you follow the other person's lead in all oral communication, if you develop the skill to pick up clues to feelings by paying attention to facial expressions, gestures, and so on, you will have no trouble. These clues are called nonverbal communication. They will often tell you more about a person's feelings than the spoken word. One final point: Listen actively when talking with your supervisors.

Talking With Workers Under Your Supervision

When you are promoted to a supervisory position of any kind, such as supervisor, chief clerk, or executive assistant, your role is reversed. Now it is important that you put your staff members at ease. Of course, the best way to put another person at ease is to feel relaxed yourself. Even when you have started up the ladder of success, you should still be yourself. You should not try to imitate the speech, the mannerisms, the style of someone higher up the ladder than you are. Remember, too, the importance of a positive attitude toward those whose work you supervise. If you honestly like your staff members, they will know it. Your communication will be easier. In addition to feeling positively toward your staff members, you should tell them you appreciate their good work. Everyone needs recognition; give it when you can.

When it is necessary to make a comment about work that is not good, try the device of getting the worker to talk. Ask questions about the work. If your feeling is positive, if you have given praise when it is deserved, your task of constructive criticism will not be so difficult. Always remember, however, that criticism must be for the action, not for the person. You never say, "You must be really dumb not to follow these simple directions!" Instead, you might say, "Did you understand the directions for making out the sales slips? If you did, I must ask you what happened with these slips that were filled out yesterday." Notice, in the latter example, that the slips become the villain— not the worker. This point is an important one. Avoid direct accusations. Saying *you* when you praise and not saying *you* when you give blame is a skill worth cultivating.

Aids to Communication

As you communicate with others, you may either talk or listen. When you listen, you are the receiver. When you talk, you are the sender. The following aids to effective communication apply specifically to the activity of sending. You *send* the communication when you speak or write.

Be Specific

In either speaking or writing you will *send* more effectively if you deal in specifics, if you avoid generalities. General statements are uninteresting mainly because they are hard to picture in your mind. Writing or speaking about a college, for example, you might picture a red brick building covered with ivy and think, "Central College." Using the words, "Central College," the person reading or listening to your message would probably get the same mental picture. What will your reader or listener picture, however, if you write or say, "college"? The words "Yale University" may appear in the mental picture. The word "college" is not as concrete as the name of the specific college. If you write or say "school," you are still more abstract, since your reader or listener may visualize an elementary school. If you write or say "institution," you climb to still another level of abstraction, since your reader or listener may now visualize a hospital or even a jail.

The way to avoid abstract words is to ask yourself one or more of the five W's—Who, Where, When, Why (or How), and What. If you are tempted to say "charitable organization," you would ask yourself, "What charitable organization?" and your answer might be the Red Cross. The listener certainly would get a clearer picture from the words Red Cross than from "charitable organization."

Be Clear

To communicate clearly means that the reader or listener gets the message you send. Your message will be received correctly only if you make your statement or request so clear that it cannot be misunderstood. Following are three devices that can be recommended with confidence to help you speak or write clearly.

Brevity. The reader or listener will understand five words better than ten words. Ten will be better understood than twenty. In the same way, a two-syllable word will be better understood than a six-syllable word. A paragraph containing six lines will be easier to understand than one containing twelve lines. Brevity must not be overdone, of course, since your communication must be grammatically correct and appropriately phrased. Within these limits, though, your communication will be clearer if you use short words, short sentences, and short paragraphs.

Variety. Your communication will get attention if you avoid sameness, such as several sentences beginning the same way. Another way to put variety into what you say or write is to avoid using the same words or phrases over and over. Watch, too, a tendency to write several sentences in succession that all start in the same way, as well as that of having all of your sentences the same length. Interest and clarity will be improved if you have variety in the way you make up your sentences.

Itemization. Clarity is improved if you itemize any sort of list that you wish to communicate. Notice how hard it is to understand the following written instructions: Please go to the files and find the letter we wrote to J. K. Bliss last Monday and then make two Xerox copies and send one of them to the auditing department and the other one to the central filing department, and to the one to the filing department attach a copy of the contract signed by Bliss in October of last year.

By itemizing these instructions, their clarity is improved, as follows: Will you please (1) make two Xerox copies of the letter sent to J. K. Bliss on Monday, October 5; (2) make a copy of the contract signed by Bliss in October of last year; (3) send one copy of the letter and a copy of the contract to the central filing department; and (4) send the other copy of the letter to the auditing department.

The instructions are even easier if the writer lists the items one below the other, as follows:

Will you please take care of the following:

1. Make two Xerox copies of the letter to J. K. Bliss on October 5 of this year.
2. Make a Xerox copy of the Bliss contract signed in October of last year.
3. Send one copy of the letter and a copy of the contract to the central filing department.
4. Send the other copy of the letter to the auditing department.

Be Positive

You have learned how important it is to be positive in earlier chapters. As you will see, it is just as important to write or to take care of business matters over the telephone in a positive manner. In other words, it is better to say what you *can* do instead of what you *cannot* do. When you must say, "No," however, one of the following ways will help you.

Imply The Negative. If someone asks you, as manager of a mail order company, for copies of your sales letters, you might answer, "Since our company depends wholly on sales

and collection letters for its business, they are for our use only."
Such an answer strongly *implies* that the answer is "No," yet it
does not actually say "No."

Say What You Can Do. Another device for handling negatives is to avoid the "No" by saying what you can do. For example, a customer may call you to ask if a Christmas order can
be moved forward and shipped on December 1. Instead of answering that early shipment is impossible, you might say, "We'll
have your order to you by December 15—with seven shopping
days still remaining before Christmas."

Use Sentence Structure. If you must say "No," the sting
can be removed somewhat by putting the "No" in the dependent
clause of the sentence, the part of the sentence that cannot stand
alone. Instead of saying, "You failed to send the catalog number
of the camera you wanted," you would say, "If you will give
me the catalog number of your camera, I'll send it right out."

Impersonalize The Negative. Your "No" answer will be
more acceptable if a *thing* (rather than the person) is the subject
of your sentence. By saying "This tire appears to have failed
on the sidewall," the listener will accept your statement. But
if you say, "What did you do—run this tire into a curb?" your
statement sounds accusing and your listener will not accept it.
Still another way to impersonalize the negative is to put the
listener or reader in a group. To get a newly-employed TV service
technician to always check a particular circuit, it could be stated
in the following way: "Our service people have found that, by
checking this circuit first, a lot of time can be saved when trouble-
shooting the loss of video." Such a statement would encourage
the new person to follow the correct procedure without being
harsh.

Speaking Before Groups

If you are given an assignment to speak to a group—a com-
mittee, a club, an organization—your procedure will be similar
to that used in writing. You collect your thoughts in written
form, organize them, and write and rewrite your outline. But
there is a difference. When you prepare a talk, it is usually best

Illus. 13–3. Listen to a recording of your voice to determine your speaking faults.

Photo by Peggy Palange, University of Cincinnati

to stop at the outline stage. Some good speakers, it is true, write down their speeches and memorize them. But those who speak frequently seem to do better if they first outline their thoughts carefully and then speak from the outline. One reason for this is that effective reading is even more difficult than effective speaking. Unless you have been trained in reading aloud, you will give a dull and uninteresting presentation if you rely on reading alone. If you are a "just starting" speaker, the following tips may be helpful.

Notes for Speaking

Type your notes on 5″ × 8″ white cards instead of on regular sheets of paper. Cards can be handled so that the audience is less likely to notice them. Sheets of paper will be noticed as you turn each page. If you use stories, dramatic statistics, or other examples (and they are good to use), type them on yellow cards of the same size. The use of colored cards signals the fact that the example is coming up and helps you get ready for a change in your approach. It is also a good idea to write on the back of each example card the date and title of the talk in which it was used. This technique will help you avoid using the same example before the same group another time.

Tips for Improving Your Speaking

To improve your speaking ability, two attributes are needed: relaxation and practice.

Relaxation. Learn to relax your throat. Yawn. Notice how your throat feels. When you yawn, your throat is open. Try to keep this feeling when you are speaking. If you learn to relax, you will benefit in another way. That same sense of relaxation will be conveyed to your audience, helping them to listen more easily.

Space Fillers. The nervous speaker punctuates remarks with "uh" and "er." To break the "uh-er" habit, in addition to relaxing, you should just stop speaking when you are at a loss for a word. Pause, look pleasant, and no one will know the difference. In fact, a pause is actually helpful, since many of us speak too fast.

Another bad conversational habit is the excessive use of "you know," or "y'know." By continually using "y'know" in your conversation, you may cause the listener to quit listening. After all, if the listener already knows what you are saying, then why listen? "Do you know?" is an honest question. "Y'know" is a bad habit.

Practice. Take advantage of every opportunity you have to talk with others. *Want* to share, to communicate. Next, listen to a recording of your voice. You may not recognize what you hear as belonging to you, but you will probably note certain faults that you can improve. Some possible faults are these:

Do you project your voice? If you want to be a good speaker, you must "push" your voice to the person farthest away from you. Learn to speak directly to the ones in the back row.

Do you speak with your best pitch? There is a simple test for finding your best pitch. Go to a piano and sing "ah" down the scale to your lowest comfortable pitch. Then sing back up four whole notes. This level is your best speaking pitch. Most of us speak with a higher pitch than is pleasing.

Does your voice sound alive? If you are interested and enthusiastic about what you are saying, you will be interesting—and your voice will sound vibrant and alive.

Do you speak your words clearly? Speaking clearly results in proper articulation. This quality is improved if you pronounce your consonants sharply.

Do you look at your audience? Your listeners will be much more interested in what you have to say if you look directly at them. Looking at your audience is called "eye contact." It means that you look at someone's face in the center of your audience for a short time, then at someone's face on one side of your audience, then at someone's face on the other side. Never devote all your attention to just one part of your audience, since this makes those in the other areas feel left out (and they will tune *you* out). Also remember that looking at the walls above their heads will not do. And *never* look out of the window while you are speaking.

Questions and Projects

1.   Listen to the radio or television speech of any well-known personalities and bring to class a list of their colorful words, of their specific words, or of the words they pronounce differently from the way you are accustomed to hearing them.

2.   Locate an article in a current newspaper or magazine bearing on a current problem, and underline the words that give the article color and life.

3.   On a separate sheet of paper, substitute more colorful expressions for these trite ones:

pale as a ghost	busy as a bee
green as grass	sweet as sugar
pure as snow	white as a sheet

4.   Reread the first four suggestions for eliminating faults in your speaking: (Do you project your voice? Do you speak with your best pitch? Does your voice sound alive? Do you speak your words clearly?)

For one week spend 10 or 15 minutes a day on *one* fault that is most serious for you. For example, if you lack projection, count from *one* to *ten* aloud, starting softly on *one* and increasing your projection until it is at its strongest point on the count of ten.

5. To increase your vocabulary, try the following plan of learning a new word each week.

    a. Choose a word from your daily reading that you do not know.
    b. Place this word, including pronunciation and meaning, on your bulletin board, chalkboard, or attach it to your mirror, where you will see it several times a day.
    c. Involve your family or friends in the activity.
    d. Use the new word in your speaking; perhaps others will use the word, too.
    e. Remember: Each week choose a new word—but don't forget the new words you learned earlier. Keep a list of all the words you have worked on, and make them a part of your daily speech.

6. How would you start a conversation with the following people:

    a) your supervisor
    b) a co-worker
    c) the president of your firm
    d) a prospective client or customer

Case Problems

1.   The Customer is Always Right.

Louis Welti works in the office of the sales department of a coffee company. He keeps the records of the salespeople who are on the city routes. His books show the supplies the salespeople take out of stock and their returns in cash and merchandise. Louis is exceptionally efficient. If there is a mistake in the record of a route person, Louis always catches it. If there is an argument about reports, Louis can offer the needed facts to eliminate further confusion. Louis does have one fault; he has not developed a courteous telephone technique. The manager has had a number of complaints from customers who are annoyed at the way Louis handles situations over the telephone. The following are typical of Louis' conversations:

> An irate customer says, "I told the salesperson I wanted a light roast and I got a package of dark roast instead." Louis answers, "Why don't you give the dark roast a try? It's one of our best sellers."

A dissatisfied customer says, "I just received my bill and you have charged me $10.16 for Saturday, November 18. I did not place or receive an order on that date." Louis says, "You must be mistaken. The bills are checked most carefully before we send them out."

An angry customer says, "I asked that my orders be delivered on Saturday morning, and this is the third time they have been sent out on Monday." Louis says, "This is the first time I have heard about it. Are you sure you told the delivery clerk?"

When the office manager speaks to Louis about the complaints he has received, Louis defends himself vigorously. He knows he is right; he says he is positive the customers are mistaken. The next time, the office manager has to come to the rescue to keep a battle from developing and resolves to tell Louis what he should have said in each of the cases cited.

1. Assuming that you are the office manager, how would you have answered each of the three customers?
2. Why does Louis talk as he does? Do you think he may be covering up a lack of confidence?
3. What personal techniques should Louis develop in addition to keeping records?

2. What About English Mechanics?

Barbara Chamberlain works for a construction company. In her letters, she is very careless about her English usage. Such matters as grammar and old-fashioned phrasing seem of no importance to her. George Madsen, a young man who works in the office under Barbara's supervision, has always done well in English courses in school. He has also done quite well in a course in business communication.

1. Should George do anything about this situation?
2. Should Barbara be expected to learn and use better English skills?
3. If George decides to correct the mistakes in grammar, how far should he go in changing his supervisor's style or characteristic way of expressing her meaning?

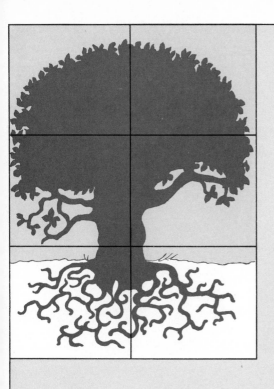

PART SIX
Working

Chapter 14
Your job campaign

If you want to find the right job, you should work at it. It may take several weeks of continuous effort. You should keep in mind that you are at an important point in your career and should avoid the temptation to accept the first job offer that comes your way. Take your time; work hard at each step in the process. You will then be much more likely to find a job that gives you personal satisfaction. Since you are actually marketing your skills, knowledge, ability, and personal qualities, you must learn all you can about them or, in effect, about yourself.

Sources of Job Information

It was near graduation time and Gregory and Janice were talking about the future. Janice said, "I know I want to work in accounting, but I haven't the faintest idea about where to start looking for a job. I don't even know if there are any jobs out there for me." "I know just how you feel," Gregory responded. "I've been looking at newspaper ads for people in advertising, but there's not much there. And I can't tell if I have what it takes for those jobs anyway."

After you have analyzed the product (yourself), you must analyze the market (the job available). Look over your own qualifications again. What other possible lines of work do they suggest? After you have settled on two or three alternative lines

Illus. 14–1. Your Job Campaign: Analyze the Market and Your Own Qualifications

of work, the next step is to look around for one or more specific jobs. There are a number of sources where you might inquire: school placement services, newspaper want ads, state and federal merit tests, public employment bureaus, and private employment agencies.

School Placement Services

Larger schools now have job development specialists concerned with placing students. The placement officer will ask you to fill out an application blank or data sheet. Then this person will interview you and will consult the references you provide. This is an excellent source for you to consider. Business people who have had good results with school placement services are glad to use their services again.

Your school placement officer will probably keep a file with information about you that employers might want. This file may include letters of reference from your former teachers or employers. A letter of reference allows someone who knows you to recommend you to potential employers. The letter provides first-hand information about your work habits, personality, skills, and potential for success in the jobs for which you might apply. Most employers expect to be provided with references and often use them as a basis for their hiring decisions. One caution should be given in connection with the use of references. Always ask others if you may use their names as references. This is a courtesy to your reference, but it is also good insurance for you. Teachers, particularly, have so many students in one year that they may be grateful for the opportunity to renew your acquaintance. This, in turn, will make it possible for them to give you a more detailed recommendation.

Small schools may not have placement services. This does not mean, however, that you should not keep in touch with your former school in such cases. Placing of graduates in small schools may be handled by vocational teachers, the teacher in charge of the work experience program, the school counselor, or by the principal. Ask your former teacher whom you should consult, then go to this person and leave your name and your qualifications and references.

Your responsibility does not end (in either the formal or informal placement situation) with the interview. You should cooperate with the placement person by following up leads at once. If the placement person receives word that a job is available at 9 a.m., it may be taken by 2 p.m. A second need for promptness lies in reporting the results of your job interview with the placement person. If you are given the job, no other applicants should be sent for it; if you were late in applying and the job was taken, you should give the placement person this information. If you did not get the job and it is still open, the placement person will want to send other applicants. Also, you should be referred to other positions.

Newspaper Want Ads

You should always take advantage of the help wanted ads in your daily newspapers. These are not only a source of openings; they also show a trend as to the type of openings most prevalent. If you are undecided between two possible areas of work, for example, a study of the available jobs listed in the help wanted section should tip the scales in favor of the one providing the best opportunities. Further help can be found in the want ads; namely, the level of competence needed. A short-order cook may have to show previous cooking training or experience. In the secretarial field, for example, the majority of the ads may specify 60 words a minute in typewriting and 100 words a minute in shorthand dictation. Mechanics may need to be certified.

There are two ways of replying to a help wanted ad. If an address is given, you must go in person for an interview. If a box number is given, you must reply with a data sheet and an application letter. (These topics are discussed later in this chapter.)

State and Federal Civil Service Tests

Two excellent sources of jobs are the federal civil service and state civil service. If you are interested in either of these opportunities, you should inquire at the respective offices in each case. Federal civil service tests are given frequently throughout the year. The dates and places of these tests can be secured at your federal building or post office, either in person or by letter. Information concerning state examinations can be obtained at your state capitol.

Public Employment Bureaus

The United States Employment Service conducts tests, arranges interviews, and provides job leads without charge. This service was established in 1933. Agencies are located in the larger cities of all the states. Most local agencies are referred to as Job Service Centers. At the state level the agency is typically called the Division of Employment and Training. Your local Job Service Center is an excellent employment agency and one that merits your acquaintance. Businesses using the USES turn the screening of applicants over to the agency. Two or three applicants considered best suited for a certain position are then sent to the firm requesting help. Beginners in business, especially, will do well to visit their public employment bureau to learn about the services offered.

Private Employment Agencies

In addition to the public employment services, there are many private agencies operating in most cities. These agencies do charge a fee for placement. In some cases the applicant is expected to pay this fee (which involves a certain percentage of the salary received in the first months of employment), but, in many cases, the new employer pays the fee. The advantage of the private agency may rest on the fact that these agencies often specialize in certain types of jobs. One may specialize in placing executives, others may place clerical workers, and so on. With such specialization, of course, the agency should have a deeper knowledge of the field covered and may have the exact job for a certain applicant.

Your Data Sheet

Perhaps the most important single job-finding aid is your data sheet. Whether you apply for a job on your own, or whether you are asked by an executive of a firm to come in for an interview, your cause will be aided if you have a neatly typed data sheet to submit.

To be effective, your data sheet must "put your best foot forward." Make *it* look as good as *you* do. One reason for the popularity of the data sheet is the ease with which it can be scanned by the interviewer. It is also helpful for the firm hiring you to keep the data sheet in your personnel file. When opportunities for advancement arise, your data sheet will provide, in concise form, the information that will help them make a choice.

A data sheet is an outline of information that should be of interest to an employer, arranged attractively under headings. After listing your full name, address, phone number, and social security number, the headings in your data sheet should include the following: Personal Information, Education, Work Experience (or Experience With People if you have not yet worked), and References.

Social Security Number

You may already have your Social Security card. If not, you should get one because your Social Security number is required by all employers. It is the identification number for your wages and contributions to the Social Security program. It is a good idea to memorize your number and keep your card in a safe place.

Personal Information

Some data sheets begin with personal details or vital statistics, such as age, height, weight, health, hobbies, and marital status. You may list a minimum of organization memberships in this section. You should be aware that there is some information that the employer may want, but which cannot be required. Legally, your race, sex, marital status, religion, age, or handicap may not be considered as reasons for refusing to hire you. However, you can provide any information *you choose* to reveal. If you provide this information, along with a photograph of yourself, many employers appreciate it. The heading, Personal Information, should be underscored; and other titles should be followed by a colon, as follows:

Personal Information

Age:	23	Health:	Excellent
Height:	5'3"	Marital Status:	Single
Weight:	120 lbs.		

Education

When you list your education, you should list first the last school you attended, with your major field of study and the date of your graduation. For example:

1979–81	Michigan State University Lansing, MI	B.S. (With Distinction) Accounting
1978–79	Lansing Community College Lansing, MI	Certificate Program Legal Secretary
1974–78	Okemos High School Okemos, MI	High School Diploma

Work Experience

In listing your experience, it is best to be quite specific. Such statements as, "Worked in grocery store," do not give enough information. Dates, names of companies and employers, plus a description of the work, are needed. Another important point is to list the jobs you have held in reverse order (the last job first). Following is an example, assuming you have worked in two different jobs:

1980–81	Payroll clerk for Mr. Thomas A. Jennings, Manager, General Electronics, Inc., Minneapolis, MN; part-time while attending college.
1979–80	Timekeeper for Ms. H. M. Wells, Project Engineer, Wells Construction Company, Springfield, IL; worked summers for three years.

If you have held more than five different jobs, it is best to choose only the latest ones or the most important ones. The experience section of your data sheet is to show concisely that you have done satisfactory work, that you know what it means to do a day's work for a day's pay. The listing of additional positions adds nothing new and takes up valuable space that can be better used in other ways.

Experience With People

If you have never had a job, full-time or part-time, the work experience section of your data sheet is headed, Experience

With People. Here you should list organizations to which you belong. Of particular interest to employers are leadership activities in debating, campus newspapers and literary organizations, athletics, and class offices. It is believed that such activities identify a person who can communicate well and who has learned to work as a part of a team. These qualities are vitally needed in the working world.

References

The last section of your data sheet should contain the names, titles, and addresses of three or four individuals who can recommend your work, your scholarship, and/or your character. These should be arranged attractively. Some employment agencies recommend omitting specific references and writing instead, after the heading, "References furnished on request."

References

Mr. Thomas A. Jennings	Ms. H. M. Wells
Manager	Project Engineer
General Electronics, Inc.	Wells Construction Company
1067 Main Street	1549 Somerset Road
Minneapolis, MN 55435–1542	Springfield, IL 62707–1709
Dr. Morton L. Smith	Dr. Harriet Sholund
Professor of Economics	Business Department
Cutler College	Cutler College
Minneapolis, MN 55433–1542	Minneapolis, MN 55433–1542

Interviewing for the Job You Want

> Janice and Gregory were having lunch in the school cafeteria. "I must have filled out a dozen job applications in the last two weeks," said Janice. "Now I have an appointment with the personnel manager at Ajax. I'm petrified!" "You mean you're afraid to talk about yourself?" "Yes, and I have no idea what will be asked. If I appear to be nervous, I'll look stupid. When you're in competition for a job in accounting, that can be a disaster." "Don't worry," said Gregory. "Just remember everything we learned about interviewing. You'll do OK!"

Illus. 14–2. Avoid tension on an interview by ignoring the possible results.

You may have heard that the interview is the place where you should put your best foot forward. However, if you try too hard to make a good impression, the impression you make may be one of effort, of strain. Of course, your first interview may be rather frightening. Any first experience has its hazards. One sure way to make it more frightening than it need be, however, is to worry about what may happen. Don't even think about the success or lack of success in your first interview. Instead, consider your interview to be a pleasant conversation in which you will do your best to answer all questions promptly and correctly. Also, be ready to ask questions of your own when the opportunity arises and try to appear at ease.

Why is it important to refrain from looking ahead to the probable results of your interview? The answer is contained in one word, *tension*. If you are concerned with the results of what you are saying, of the success or failure of the impression you are making, you will become tense. Tension causes all kinds of unfortunate reactions. Your memory fails you; you hesitate in answering the simplest questions, thus appearing to be unsure of your answers; your expression, your voice, your posture, all advertise that you are frightened. All of this can be eliminated if you concentrate on the *now* rather than on the *future*. Resolve to do your best, but decide before you begin that the first two or three interviews will be for the sole purpose of learning how to be your own real self in a new situation.

If you can eliminate tension by being relaxed, you will be able to show the real you to your interviewer—something you will not be able to do if you are tense. After all, your interviewer will appreciate your relaxed attitude. It is not pleasant to inspire fear in people you talk with, and your interviewer does not enjoy this any more than you do. Your interview will be much more successful if you are relaxed and if you are prepared.

After seeing you in person, your interviewer will want evidence of your abilities. The reason your abilities come second is that your appearance is infinitely easier for your interviewer to evaluate. The way you appear will provide some idea of the way you will work. These estimates will be supplemented with questions and, possibly, tests. When questions are asked, general statements of what you like to do, of your interest in people, and so on are of little help. A company wants to hire workers who have proved themselves. You may feel that you have no proof and, when you seek your first job, you may feel completely inadequate. What you may not realize, though, is that experienced interviewers understand this feeling; they consider it natural. What they will not understand is any attempt on your part to "gild the lily." If you have had absolutely no previous experience, you must state this frankly when asked. You must not pretend to be something you are not.

An interviewer is interested, however, in any kind of work you may have done. Although you may be applying for office work, the interviewer will be glad to know about newspaper routes, care of young children, playground directing, leadership in summer camps, manual labor, and any other forms of work you may have performed. Vacation spent in worthwhile work also tells your interviewer that you have formed desirable work habits.

What You Can Do For a Specific Company

Before you go to any company for an interview, learn all you can about it. Find out what products are manufactured or sold, what services are performed, and the location of branch offices in other cities. Ask your librarian for indexes containing this information. You may be surprised to know how much information is available to you. Whether you have an opportunity to display this knowledge is not too important. What is important is the confidence you will gain when you succeed in becoming acquainted with the company.

When you know something about the company, you will be better prepared to display what you can do. First, gather together samples of your work. If you are young and inexperienced, you may not have many exhibits to present. What you do put into your collection (or portfolio), however, should be of the highest quality. Depending on the kind of job for which you are applying, you should gather exhibits that will show you are familiar with the type of work done in the company. Actual evidence is much more effective than any unsupported statement you could make.

Take a Deep Breath

No matter how well prepared you may be, the effect will be ruined if you appear for your interview looking as though you just barely made it. Allow yourself twice as much time to get to your destination than you would normally require. Then an unexpected delay will not create a problem for you. *And always go to your interview alone.* Any young person who needs the support of a friend is likely to appear too immature to take a job.

When you go into the reception room of the company, give your name and the time of your appointment (and the name of the interviewer if you know it). The receptionist will probably ask you to be seated and wait. Don't be alarmed if there are other people waiting, too. Be friendly, reply to all questions courteously, but do not bother the receptionist or other employees with questions.

Even if you wait for some time, try to relax; think of a pleasant subject. Above all, don't anticipate difficulties when your turn comes to go in to talk with the interviewer. Even with the best of intentions, you may find yourself suffering from stage fright as you walk into a strange office. It may help you to know that stage fright often acts as an aid to the sufferer. "Butterflies" may mean that you are keyed up to a high level of alertness, and your first words to the interviewer will get rid of your nervousness. In any case, the following suggestions may help you.

Stand Tall. The first impression you make is certain to be a better one if you stand straight and tall. This does not mean a stiff military posture, however. Raise your chest, keep your ears lifted, and your posture will be as it should be. One hazard that may occur: the interviewer may be busy when you go into the office. If this should happen, do nothing except stand quietly until you are spoken to. Don't do anything with your hands as you stand. Putting your hands in your pockets or even crossing your arms all advertise that you are ill at ease. Just let your hands hang at your sides. Regardless of how this feels to you, it looks more relaxed than any other attitude you could assume.

Think About Something Pleasant. Have you ever had someone ask you to look pleasant as your picture was being taken? Was the smile you forced a natural one? Probably not, yet this is usually the way any attempt to look pleasant turns out.

A better way to achieve the appearance of being comfortable in your surroundings is to think of something pleasant. If you do this, your "look" will follow suit, and it will also appear more natural. Perhaps the best thing to think about is some good point you have noticed about the company. If you are interested, you will look interested—and this is a pleasant sight for the interviewer to see. It can set the tone of the entire interview and contribute to your getting the job.

What Should You Say First? Suppose you have been standing in front of the interviewer's desk for several moments waiting to be recognized. What should you say? Remember, the interviewer does not know you; so the first thing you say is your name. In your most natural manner, tell the interviewer who you are—and use the interviewer's name. Say, "Mr. Eccles,

I am John Cardwell. You asked me to come in this morning."
It is pretentious to give yourself any title whatever, so don't
say you are Mr. Cardwell or Miss Ellsworth. And don't supply
your middle name unless you normally go by both names. It
sounds all right to say, "I am Mary Jo Smith, Mr. Eccles," but
to say, "Mr. Eccles, I am John Kennleworth Cardwell," is too
much. After you give your name, the interviewer will probably
ask you to be seated.

What do you do with your belongings? In cold weather,
it is best to leave your outer coat, boots, or other paraphernalia
in the reception room, hanging them up if there is some arrangement such as hooks, hat racks, or closets available. It is definitely
awkward to carry excess clothing into the interviewer's office.
If you are asked to write something, do so at your chair. Do
not touch the interviewer's desk. Don't put anything on it, and
don't look at anything on it (letters, contracts, and the like). If
you can keep your hands quiet, you will add to the good impression you make. Any kind of activity of the hands, turning a
ring, smoothing your hair, touching your face, will show that
you are nervous.

What Do You Say?

The interviewer should lead the interview, but this may
be done in several different ways. Some interviewers ask many
questions. When this happens, be sure to answer with enough
detail. For example, if an interviewer should say, "You say your
name is John Cardwell," you might answer, "Yes." A more detailed answer is better, however. If you continue, "Mr. Kent
from the Central College Placement Office asked me to see you,"
this places you more exactly than merely answering "Yes." This
answer, too, can naturally lead into a discussion of your school
work, the subjects you like best, your grades in your major field,
school activities, and so on.

It is important that you answer all questions without hesitation. You may be asked why you want to work for this particular
company. Such a question is frequently asked, so it is wise to
be ready with an answer. If you have a friend who is employed
in the company, this is a valid reason. Or you may answer that
you are interested in this particular business field (banking,
manufacturing, the oil business, or whatever it may be). Another

Illus. 14-3. Answer all interview questions honestly and without hesitation.

reason may be that you have been a customer of the company and have admired the way they deal with the public. Whatever your reason may be, give it promptly and sincerely.

Controversial Questions. Some interviewers make a practice of asking a question or two that is controversial. Such a question might have to do with politics, religion, racial matters, or economics. If this kind of question is asked you, give a mild, but straightforward answer. It is important that you refrain from anything that may sound argumentative no matter what your interviewer may say. It is possible that such questions are asked to see if the applicant can remain calm under pressure. No matter what the motive, however, it will be to your advantage if you do remain calm.

Your Previous Employer. You must avoid saying anything negative about a former employer or teacher. Your interviewer may assume that you will be just as likely to criticize this company to someone else. The reputation for loyalty is built up by saying positive things about former associates of all kinds. Since no one wants to hire a troublemaker, an employer will avoid hiring a person who whines or complains. Saying negative things about former associates is one symptom of the trouble-making habit. Be careful that you keep away from any possibility of having the tag of troublemaker applied to you.

What About Salary? Should the beginning applicant say anything about salary? In general, it is best not to bring up the matter too soon. Don't ask the interviewer how much the job is worth at the beginning of the interview. On the other hand, you should be prepared with some statement about salary if the question is asked you. What should you say if the interviewer asks, "What salary do you expect?" If you are currently employed or if you have worked recently, you might mention the salary you made or are making. The beginner, however, does not have this advantage.

What should you say if you are seeking your first job? In this case, you need not mention a specific amount. You might say you are interested in advancement, but that the interviewer would have more of an idea what the particular job is worth. This statement would open the matter for discussion.

Before you go to your first interview, you should find out what beginning jobs are paying in your community. Possible sources of information about salaries are your school placement service, the United States Employment Service, and teachers in your school. If you should reach the end of your interview and find that nothing has been said about salary, you will have to bring up the subject. You might say, "Could you give me some idea of the salary?" Stated this way, the question sounds reasonable rather than grasping. It should merit a factual reply.

When discussing salary, you should be perfectly frank. Do not say you have been offered some amount if it is not the case. The quickest way to be blacklisted in the world of work is to misrepresent facts when applying for a job. If you should be seriously considered for employment, your would-be employer will certainly check on the information you have given. On the other hand, you should not understate your desires. If you are willing to work for the salary suggested, that is one thing; it is another if you agree to the suggested salary in order to get the job and then regret your decision.

Remember that a business is not a charitable organization. You should not explain why you need a job or why you need a certain salary. The employer is interested in what you can do for the company. It is much better, then, for you to emphasize your abilities and skills, your knowledge of the work to be done, and your interests in the field.

You Fill Out An Application Blank. One customary activity when being interviewed by a firm is filling out an application for employment. Again, do not hurry. Take enough time to read each item carefully. Notice if your name is to be written or printed and whether your last or first name is to appear first. Unless you are asked to typewrite the information, the blank should be filled out in longhand. Careful reading of each statement will eliminate erasures. You should answer all questions, leaving no blank spaces. If the question does not apply to you, draw a horizontal line in the space provided. This indicates that you have read the question but that it does not apply to you. If you leave a blank space, this could mean that you failed to see the question or that you did not wish to answer it for some reason.

Be as neat as you can, both in writing and in keeping the blank free from smudges, wrinkles, and fingerprints. Be extra careful to carry out all directions that are printed on the blank. Some firms consider the ability to follow directions one of the best indications of the applicant's suitability for employment.

You Take Tests. In a way, an interview can be a miniature working situation. You may be given a test that simulates the work for which you are applying. Remain calm, concentrate, and do your best. Do not worry about "failing" or "passing." And above all, do not try to fake anything or misrepresent yourself.

You Leave Promptly. When you have finished taking any tests that are required and have filled in the required forms, and when the interviewer has asked everything needed, there should be some indication that the interview is over. This indication may be a statement, a question, or merely a long pause.

You must be perceptive enough to catch your cue, whatever it is and act upon it at once. Long, drawn-out leave-takings are inappropriate and will do you harm. You should pick up your belongings, rise, thank the interviewer for considering you, say good-bye pleasantly, and then go. There is one thing you might make sure of, however. The interviewer may say that you will be called in a few days after your references have been consulted. If nothing is said, you may ask if it will be all right if you call in a week or so to see if a decision has been reached. In any case, whether you mention the matter or not, following up on a job you want is good strategy because it will indicate to the prospective employer that you have a sincere interest in getting the job.

You Follow Up. It is courteous to write a short letter of appreciation for the interview. Then, after several days, you may call the interviewer and ask if the position for which you applied has been filled. If the job is still open, the telephone call may bring attention to your application; if it is filled, knowing about it at once is better than waiting and wondering. Some excellent jobs have been won because of persistent follow-up on the part of the applicant.

Keeping yourself in the picture is usually to your advantage; but whatever happens, you must not give up. You will learn a great deal from going on several interviews. If you consider each interview as a stepping-stone to the job you want, you will be less likely to try too hard to impress any one employer. Just be yourself; it is the most impressive *you* that you can present.

Questions and Projects

1. It has been said that if you work at getting a job for two weeks, eight hours a day, as hard as you would *on* the job, you will get the job. Outline two weeks of activities on a job-finding campaign that would bring this kind of success.

2. How many businesses can you name in your community where you might apply for a job you would like?

3. Survey 10 business firms regarding the future openings for some kind of work that you can do. Present your findings to the class orally.

4. If you had your choice, in what business would you like to work? How many such businesses are there in your community? Prepare a summary if requested by your instructor.

5. Suppose you were being interviewed today. On a separate sheet of paper, make a chart like the one below. In the space provided, write the adjective that would best describe the way an interviewer would probably rate you in the following:

Appearance	_____	Attitude	_____
Approach	_____	Temperament	_____
Dress	_____	Knowledge	_____
Hands and face	_____	General reaction	_____
Speech	_____		

Case Problems

1. If at First You Don't Succeed . . .

Carla Mendoza is about to graduate from the junior college in her town and has begun her job-getting campaign. On Tuesday morning she mails ten application letters with data sheets enclosed to the leading firms in the area. On Friday there is one reply. The office manager of Stewart Electronics, Inc. asks her to call for an appointment for an interview. Carla calls and is told to come in the following Monday. When Carla arrives, she is told that Chris McKay, the office manager, has been called out of town for a week. Carla asks if there is someone else she can see, but the receptionist answers that no one else in the firm can hire new employees. Greatly discouraged, Carla goes back to her typewriter and sends out ten more application letters.

1. If you were Carla, what would you have done in this situation?
2. Which would you consider the most effective follow-up in this case, a letter, a telephone call, or a personal call at the office the following week? Why?
3. Why might Carla take the initiative, even though she did not break the appointment?
4. What attitude should Carla take when she sees Chris McKay? Why?
5. Should Carla show any resentment because of the broken appointment?

2. Be Specific.

A wholesaler of carpenters' tools has a vacancy in the sales department. Jane Peterson, Director of Sales Personnel, calls the local college and asks that interested young people submit letters of application and data sheets. When the letters arrive, she narrows them down to two, one from Charles Pittman and one from Cindy Anderson. The letter from Charles Pittman contains the following as part of his third paragraph: "I am confident that I can sell tools because I am prepared to sell. I get along well with people. I believe that I can sell the tools because I have always been interested in selling. As I am going to be married soon, I am interested in a permanent job."

In the third paragraph of Cindy Anderson's letter are these statements: "I like to make bookcases and do odd jobs around the house. When you have a hobby like carpentry, you appreciate the value of Camp's forged steel tools. Although I have not sold tools, I have been a clerk in a drugstore, where I learned the techniques of selling."

1. Which person do you think Jane Peterson will employ? Why?
2. Why is it better to speak of specific facts than to make general statements when applying for a job?
3. What specific statement could Charles Pittman have written as evidence that he gets along well with people?
4. Is an approaching marriage a good selling point? Why or why not?

3. Make Your Own Opportunities.

Dale Evans and Joe Packard are good friends. Both have finished school and are ready to look for work. Both are good typists and both have studied accounting for two years. Joe feels that opportunities are limited in this town and is thinking of moving to a large city if he doesn't hear of an opening soon. Dale has no money to finance a move to a larger city and decides he will have to find something here. Consequently, he maps out a campaign. At the office of the local Chamber of Commerce, he gets a list of all of the business firms in his town that employ more than two hundred office workers. Dividing the list into geographical areas, he visits ten firms a day. At each firm he either speaks to the office manager or makes an appointment to do so later. At the end of a week, Dale has had five interviews.

1. In what ways are getting a job and selling a product from door to door similar?
2. A rule of selling is to see as many people as you can. How does this apply to finding a job?
3. It is not easy to accept a refusal. What attitude can a job applicant take toward a refusal that will help lessen its sting?
4. Are there other job sources Dale did not cover?

4. Salaries and Advancement.

Gloria Mong has applied for several jobs and has gone out on three interviews. In the first interview she found her training was not adequate; in the second, a small office, the salary was excellent; but there seemed to be no chance for advancement. The last interview is most interesting to Gloria. The job is secretary for three doctors. The beginning salary is low, but Dr. Meade (who interviews Gloria) informs her that by the end of the year the office manager, Mrs. Smott, will be retiring and, if Gloria seems capable of filling the job, she might be considered. Gloria is undecided. She dislikes refusing a good salary on what is actually just a chance that she will be offered the office manager's job six months later. She asks for a day to think the offer over.

1. Assuming that you are Gloria's friend and that she asks your advice, what would you suggest?
2. Besides salary and opportunity for advancement, is there a third consideration of even greater importance?
3. Is there a possibility that Gloria could be advanced too rapidly? Explain.
4. It is said that slow, steady progress is more likely when the ultimate job is a good one. Do you agree?

5. Experience or Change?

Ben Garcia has just graduated from high school. He has two job opportunities for the summer. One is an assembly line job in a large manufacturing company. The other, which pays more, is driving a truck. Ben likes to drive and enjoys being out of doors. He is planning to go to a nearby community college in the fall to study computer science. If you were Ben, which job would you take?

1. What advantages would each job offer? What disadvantages?
2. How should Ben rate the following three factors in choosing a summer job: salary, change of activity from school, and experience related to his chosen career?
3. Would it be better if Ben tried to find a job different from the two above? Why or why not?

Chapter 15
Moving ahead in your career

Learning to Be a Winner on the Job

Vincent had been employed for nearly two years working at the counter in an auto parts store. He liked the work but the challenge was beginning to fade. He was a bit depressed because the future in this particular position was limited. In fact, for a person with ambition and a talent for selling, it seemed like a dead-end job. And the pay was minimal. One day Vincent shared his feelings with Carol, the store manager. "I don't feel like I'm getting anywhere in this dumb job," he said. "There are no dumb jobs," Carol responded, "Only dumb people. And you're not one of them. Why don't you get your act together and start moving ahead in a career, instead of just being content to hustle car parts." "Right!" said Vincent. "Any suggestions? You're not doing so bad, Carol, so why don't you tell me the secret of your success in this business."

Why is it important for you to find and move ahead in a career that you like, that you enjoy, that adds to the best you? The answer to this question is complex, but one part of the answer lies in the number of hours you work in a day. Even with a shorter workweek, you spend more time on your job than you do in any other one activity. Those hours should add to, not subtract from, your best self. If you are happy in your hours at work, your overall mental and emotional health are enriched. If you are bored, unhappy, or filled with anxiety during those hours, the negative feelings you experience are sure to

241

Illus. 15–1. Move Ahead: Learn to Be a Winner on the Job

affect the way you live and work the rest of the day. Furthermore, your after-work hours may be filled with escape mechanisms in which you try to dull the unhappiness you have been experiencing. On the other hand, if you are happy in your work, you will find that happiness spilling into your after-work hours.

Do you feel like you are a winner or a loser? If you want to grow on the job, you must learn to feel like a winner. Part of growing on the job involves getting promoted to the next rung of the ladder. Losers seldom get promoted; therefore, you should do everything you can to show your supervisor, your co-workers, and particularly yourself that you feel like a winner. A winner keeps working on a task until it is completed. A winner has a positive attitude toward life, toward other people, and toward himself or herself.

It isn't enough to just feel like a winner, though. You must work at being a winner. Such work involves preparing for the next higher job, brushing up on your human relations skills, and learning how and when to speak up.

Which Job Should You Accept?

If you are well qualified, you may have your choice of several positions. You may be hesitant to accept a position that is available because you may think you can find a better position elsewhere. This attitude may or may not be realistic. If you cannot perform your best work with maximum satisfaction in a particular job, you are wise to discover that fact before you begin work. If you are reluctant to accept an available job because your salary or prestige demands are too great, then you may have to adjust your demands. However, as you want to build a satisfying career for yourself, you should not sell yourself short just to obtain immediate employment. Your goal is to market your services for the best possible measure of job stimulation and challenge, security, appreciation, and other rewards.

In deciding whether or not to accept a position, you should consider the following questions:

1. How stable is the firm? Is it just getting started? What are the the indications that it will succeed or grow?
2. What opportunities are there for advancement?
3. What promotional policies has the firm established?

4. Will I need more education if l remain with the firm? Have I considered plans for such education?
5. When a vacancy occurs in a better position, is someone else likely to be brought into the firm to fill the vacancy?
6. What is the reputation of this firm? Within the company itself? Among the personnel? Among customers or clients? Among other people?
7. What security does the position offer? In times of recession, what layoff policy will be followed? Can the employers usually be depended upon to be just and fair? Will the employers keep their word? If sickness takes an employee from work temporarily, will the job be filled by someone else?
8. What kind of retirement plan does the position offer? For unemployment? For sickness and hospitalization and injury?
9. Will the work be challenging enough over a period of years?
10. Do I have the aptitudes, interests, and abilities required by this job?
11. Are there any negative characteristics about the job? (Some people want to avoid night work, travel, or weekend work, for example.)

In answering these questions, you will have to find sources of information about labor trends, industrial expansion, technological changes, and other factors. Many books and magazines discuss opportunities for employment and advancement in great detail.

If You Like The Job

If you like your position, do all you can to express your appreciation by doing your best work. You may find that you can achieve greater satisfaction by growing in the present position than by competing for advancement. If you make a decision to grow in the present capacity, you must constantly try to improve your efficiency. If you have no ambition to advance or to improve in your present assignment, you will grow stale and become bored—and boring.

Length of service in a single capacity offers many rewards. By being familiar with the position, you can obtain more knowledge and skill. You will become more expert in your duties and will assume more responsibility. This thoroughness and familiarity may make you more secure in times of staff layoffs. If the human relationships in your present job are pleasant, you may find that continued work with the personnel will be more rewarding for you than adjusting to new co-workers.

Illus. 15–2. Express your appreciation for a job you like by doing your best.

GTE Telenet Communications Corp.

Some people cannot perform their best work in a competitive situation. By growth in a job instead of ambition to advance, the stress of competition can frequently be avoided, and yet a feeling of success can be accomplished.

Asking For A Raise

The ideal situation exists when true merit is recognized and need never be called to the employer's attention. If your situation is not ideal, what can you do? Obviously, there is only one answer; you must bring the matter up—you must ask for a raise. Before you speak at all, however, you must think it through very carefully first.

First, see if you are justified in asking for a promotion or a raise. If it appears that you are, make out a good case for yourself *in writing*—but be objective. What about your production? Is there a standard for your work in your position? If so, how does your production compare with this standard? What additional preparation have you made since you were hired? Have you attended extension courses? If you were to take an employment test at this point, could you score higher than on the one you took when you applied for your job?

Next, check your attitudes and work habits. Are you always prompt in arriving for work? Do you work overtime without complaint when it is necessary? How many days of work have you missed because of illness? Are you considered cooperative by your supervisor and your co-workers? When you finish the work assigned, do you find something else to do without being told?

If you feel positive about all these points, then it is time to ask your employer for an appointment. Of course, you may not want to reveal the reason for your request yet. Merely ask for an appointment. (It is a good principle of persuasive psychology to let your employer choose the day and the time.)

If your request for an appointment is granted, bring your notes with you to your interview. You might begin your remarks with something like the following: "Ms. or Mr. Blank, I have enjoyed my work here very much. As I was hired two years ago, you may be interested in the progress I have made since then." And then show how much progress you *have* made. If your statements are challenged, don't back down or get on the defensive. Simply and calmly bring up the case that you have prepared. After all, it is merely another employment interview. Remember—you passed the first one!

Finally, as in other interviews, when you have stated your case, you should thank your employer for the interview and leave. Go back to your work and be patient. Even if your employer has seemed impressed with your facts, you must not expect your raise at once. Your request may be granted after a conference with other members of the firm. Don't ruin a good case by becoming a nuisance. If you hear nothing about your request after two weeks, you might ask your employer if any decision has been made. Both when asking for a raise and following up, keep your tone friendly but impersonal.

Prepare For The Next Higher Job

One of the best times to plan for advancement is *before* you take a job. One of the considerations you should weigh is the job's promotion possibilities. A well-established firm may offer more security than advancement, for example. A new firm, on the other hand, may provide rapid advancement to those employees who are promotable material and yet be less stable than an older firm.

If you are serious about advancement, you should study the possible jobs to which you might be promoted. What other skills, abilities, and traits in addition to those you now possess are needed in the new job? Be willing to prepare yourself in these areas before asking for advancement.

Planning for advancement also means that you will develop more dependability. Be the sort of worker who completes the assigned task, no matter how dull or unchallenging it may be. If you have responsibilities (such as locking doors or closing windows), never neglect them. Follow the rules for smoking, taking coffee breaks, turning off lights. Last, and most important, do not blame others for any of your errors. Face up to your own mistakes; don't make excuses.

Flexible Goals

Another factor that helps you move ahead in your career is having an objective or goal. In today's world, however, you can be certain of one fact; our world is changing so rapidly that no one can predict the work you will be doing three years from now. You can decide on some general kind of work, something you like, something in which you have some ability. But be ready for change. You may need to retrain, even after you get your job. Some experts say the job of the future will last only two or three years before the worker will need to learn new skills.

Your goals, then, must be flexible. Moreover, they must be realistic. You must look at your abilities, your interests, your training, your work habits, and your personal qualities with an objective eye. For instance, if you can't make yourself write a letter, you should think twice about becoming a professional writer. If you have never passed a math course with a "B" or better grade, you should probably not decide to become an engineer just because engineering sounds interesting. If you don't like to take responsibility, you should not aspire to be the manager of the company.

In setting goals and planning their attainment, you cannot always be definite or specific. You can decide only the direction in which you wish to move. You can be prepared. Many opportunities you must seek for yourself. The opportunities which you will find cannot be anticipated with exactness. Some element of chance necessarily exists although you can do much to control that element of chance by training, a good record, habits of industry, and desirable personal traits. New avenues of opportunity may open to you, opportunities that you cannot now even imagine. If you have the necessary training and personal qualities, you may find employers competing to obtain your services.

Keeping Ahead of Obsolescence

The first inadequacy you may encounter when you take a new job is in your technical preparation. You may have become proficient on a certain machine, only to discover that your employer has installed another. You may find that the methods, systems, and routines of the new firm are entirely different from those you learned. What should you do?

First of all, keep a learning attitude. No matter how "sold" you may be on the equipment and procedures used in your training or your previous employment, try to adjust to those found in your present job. It will be helpful, also, if you refrain from mentioning how you solved the problem at your former school or on your other job. Like the customer, your boss is always right—at least until you have given the new situation a fair chance.

A learning attitude means that you will be alert for any departure from your present knowledge or training. Suppose your supervisor suggests that you do a certain task in a new way. Pay attention, and ask questions if you have any doubts. Write down and number each step of the new method. Ask that it be demonstrated and see if you can follow the demonstration by trying it yourself. Most supervisors prefer spending extra time with new employees rather than have errors appear in their work. Be appreciative of the extra help you receive, too. A considerate employee will find that supervisors will usually respond with equal consideration and will be glad to offer help when needed.

Illus. 15–3. Keep a learning attitude on the job.

Memorex Corporation

On-the-Job Training

Large firms may recognize the importance of the need for special training for new workers by organizing specific training courses. These may be training at the time of employment, called induction training; on-the-job training when new procedures must be learned or difficulties are encountered; and promotional training.

Induction training is usually required of all new employees, and you should be eager to learn all you can when you have such an opportunity. One vital part of such training is becoming acquainted with the overall business of the firm. Learn all you can about the product your firm manufactures or the service your firm performs. Find out about the extent of its operations and the location of its branch offices. Learning these things will result in an increased interest in your job. You will no longer be an unimportant cog in a huge machine if you realize just how your job fits into the whole.

The second type of on-the-job training may be offered to certain employees who have been transferred from other departments, those employees who lack certain needed skills, and those who are expected to work on new equipment or with new procedures. If such training is given you, welcome the opportunity to learn something new. This alone will set you apart from the other employees, as resistance to change is a common trait. Even if the training involves longer hours, be glad for the opportunity. Learning something new is a guaranteed way of improving your vigor and effectiveness. Take advantage of each opportunity that comes your way.

If, after you have been working in a firm for several years, you should be considered for advancement, you may be asked to take some sort of promotional training. Special training is usually needed before a worker is promoted to a supervisory post. If such an honor should come to you, be aware of the benefits such training will bring you. For example, you may be given help in developing your leadership qualities, in planning your work and the work of others, in developing desirable attitudes, and in evaluating your work and the work of others. This type of training is sure to be helpful to you through all your working life.

Serious Reading

Reading has been an educational tool for thousands of self-made business leaders. Regular reading for short periods of time and on one subject is the secret. If you have not developed the regular reading habit yet, decide to become knowledgeable in some area of interest to you. Get a book or two on the subject from the public library, then start reading. That's all there is to it. It will help if you set aside a special time for general reading of this type. Good reading has a further advantage, too. Teachers of writing tell us that the best way to increase your vocabulary is through reading. Such a rewarding activity should not be overlooked.

In case you have no particular interest that you care to pursue, a good start may be made by subscribing to a weekly or monthly magazine devoted to articles of general interest. Another possibility is a subscription to a business periodical. The thing to do is get started. Serious reading is an addictive habit that is good for you! It has been said, by the way, that a mind expanded never returns to its original boundaries.

Educational Courses

In some types of businesses, banking and insurance, for example, special courses are offered in community colleges and universities. College credit may be earned if it is desired. These courses provide a splendid opportunity to the ambitious worker, whether a beginner or a long-term employee.

In addition to prescribed courses, you will find adult education classes offered at many high schools as well as universities and colleges. These classes become more popular each year. In fact, many colleges have an extended day enrollment equal to that of their regular programs. The greatest increase is in training for occupations that do not require a four-year degree. One- or two-year programs leading to a certificate or an associate degree are growing in popularity and acceptance. As business continues to emphasize automation, communications, accounting, and overall improved efficiency, education beyond high school becomes more and more essential.

Still another kind of self-improvement study can be pursued through correspondence or home-study courses. These have been discussed in describing job preparation, but they are just as helpful as part of your improvement-on-the-job program. The major drawback in working by correspondence is that you must motivate yourself. Developing such self-discipline, however, is in itself a valuable accomplishment.

Ability to Change

You are adaptable to change when you are able to adjust, to alter, to fit into or respond to changing conditions. Any kind of work in business requires this trait. Your first adaptation must be to your firm. You may have worn sports clothes most of your life, yet you must change willingly to tailored clothes if your firm wishes it.

Second, you need to adapt yourself to the people around you. This includes co-workers, customers, and others with whom you must associate. You may be quick and alert in everything you do or say, yet you must talk slowly and adjust to long pauses if you wish to communicate with someone who thinks, speaks, and reacts slowly. You need to be tolerant of mistaken ideas and refrain from criticism.

A third adjustment must be made to changes in the business world. You will serve your firm best if you are constantly alert to changing routines, to changing conditions of the times, to the growth and progress of your business. The moods of customers and even the weather may require that you demonstrate your ability to adjust. If you are set in your ways, if you cling stubbornly to procedures and methods of the past, you will have failed to develop and practice adaptability. Futhermore, you will be less effective in serving your firm.

In Conclusion

In this chapter you have been encouraged to plan and move ahead in your career. Knowing yourself, taking best advantage of what you have to offer, and establishing yourself in a potentially satisfying career are among the most important tasks you face in life. The suggestions in this chapter are important if you want to be a winner. And, in a larger perspective, the many aspects of personality development presented throughout this book may be the most important preparation you can have for success in the world of work. Before you set this book aside, it might be worth your time to reread the introduction. Consider how very important your personality is as a factor in your success on the job. And finally, resolve to be more sensitive about how you should relate to other people so that the best of your personality shows through and works for you.

Questions and Projects

1. On a separate sheet of paper, draw the following scale. After you have been working for one year, ask a friend to rate you on this scale. You might suggest that you rate each other. You must both be absolutely objective in your ratings, however. Flattery will get you nowhere! If you can get an honest appraisal, and if you can work on improvement where it is needed, you will be surprised at your progress. The results of this rating should be kept and the same appraisal made a year later. A comparison of the results will show you "how you are doing." Check each item from 1 to 4 according to the following rating:

1—Good, 2—Average, 3—Fair, and 4—Needs Improvement.

		Rating
a.	Good Grooming	
b.	Cleanliness	
c.	Appropriate Dress	
d.	Dress Suits Your Personality	
e.	Color Combinations	
f.	Posture and Carriage	
g.	Correct English	
h.	Voice and Diction	
i.	Facial Expression	
j.	Poise	
k.	Health	
l.	Vitality and Enthusiasm	
m.	Self-confidence	
n.	Cheerfulness and Sense of Humor	
o.	Friendliness	
p.	Sincerity	
q.	Willingness to Cooperate	
r.	Consideration for Others	

2. Interview your supervisor, a mature co-worker, or someone who is employed in a position that you would like to hold in the future. Also, consult a counselor or librarian to obtain information from an occupational information library. With this background information, prepare a step-by-step plan for your future career. Include a brief paragraph describing each position on your career ladder. If additional educational experiences are included in your plan, describe them.

Case Problems

1. Self-Confidence?

Maria Lopez was employed by Kline's clothing store immediately upon graduation from business college. She is proud to have been chosen from the many graduates in fashion merchandising to work in such an exclusive clothing store. After five months at work, Maria is having difficulty getting along with her fellow workers and her superiors. She cannot understand why they are not impressed with her accomplishments. On several occasions she has reminded the other sales staff that she graduated with honors and was second in her class. One day Maria said to her supervisor, "Isn't it about time I left the sales floor and started doing something I have been trained for in business school? Being a salesclerk is just not giving me a chance to use my talents and abilities."

1. Why do you think Maria acts the way she does?
2. How would you answer Maria's question if you were her supervisor?
3. How do you think Maria's co-workers react to her attitude?

2. Getting Even.

Jean Miller had worked a year in a large company that employed 20 regular typists in a typing pool. During this time some of her friends had received promotions as personal secretaries to various supervisors and executives. Jean felt that she was as efficient as those who were advanced. Every time a person was promoted from the typing pool, Jean showed her resentment by sulking for a week. She knew, of course, that she should not show these negative emotions; but she wanted Jeff Share, the supervisor, to know how she felt. She had disliked Jeff Share's crisp manner from the moment she had seen him. She was sure that Jeff was doing everything he could to prevent Jean from being promoted.

You are a friend of Jean's. You have not wanted to interfere before this, but you now believe that something must be done. What would you say to Jean? Give the conversation, with the replies you believe Jean would probably make.

3. Time for Decision.

Russ Palmer has been working in the programming department of White and Charters, Inc., since he graduated from junior college a year ago. Since the time he began working with the firm he has received no raises in salary. The work of the programming department, however, has increased to the extent that two new employees have been hired to help him. This involves some supervisory work on his part. In checking the salaries paid by other firms for similar work, Russ finds that he is not earning as much as most other companies pay. As Russ is debating what to do, a friend who is office manager of Hanson and Hanson Company offers him the same type of job at 15 percent higher salary. Russ likes the people in his department, as well as the other personnel of White and Charters. Hanson and Hanson do not provide the fringe benefits he is receiving.

1. What would you do if you were Russ?
2. If you decide to ask for a raise, would you tell your employer about the other offer?

3. Write down the "case" you would present to your employer when asking for the raise.
4. In accepting a position, what factors in addition to salary should be considered?

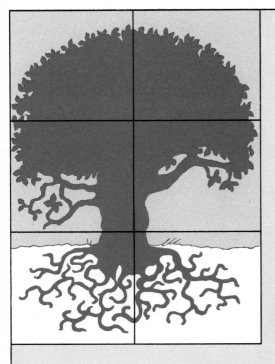

INDEX

INDEX